REVIEW FOR THE
SOCIAL STUDIES SECTION
OF THE GED TEST

By
DANIEL DONNELLY

**This book is correlated to the videotape produced by
COMEX Systems, Inc., Review for The
GED Social Studies test by
Daniel Donnelly ©2001
it may be obtained from**

comex systems, inc.

5 Cold Hill Rd.
Suite 24
Mendham, NJ 07945

Published by

comex systems, inc.
5 Cold Hill Rd., Suite 24
Mendham, NJ 07945

ISBN 1-56030-144-9

Table of Contents

The purpose of this study guide is to prepare you to take the Social Studies GED Examination. The text and questions found in this guide will not only increase your knowledge of the material covered on the examination, but also increase your confidence level. Do not plan or expect to complete this guide in one or two sittings, but rather make the time to take advantage of the information covered in it.

Before you begin working with this book, let's provide answers to some important questions you may have about this examination.

WHAT SUBJECTS WILL BE COVERED IN THIS EXAMINATION?

The social studies discipline is a varied and complex one. It includes a variety of areas, but for the GED examination the ones that you will be tested on are drawn from history, geography, economics, government, and civics.

WHAT KIND OF QUESTIONS WILL I HAVE TO ANSWER?

All of the questions will be multiple choice. The questions will be based on material that is written and/or graphical in nature. There are a total of fifty questions and you will be given eighty minutes to complete the examination.

Please note that you do not need to have a specialized knowledge in social studies, but rather possess a familiarity with the subject to do well. Your ability to use critical thinking, apply prior knowledge, and understand the written and/or graphical material will be the key to your success. Using this study guide will give you the necessary exposure to concepts, vocabulary, and important background information to increase your chances of doing well. In addition, you will be able to practice and learn from the types of questions that will be on the GED Social Studies Examination.

HOW ARE THE QUESTIONS SCORED?

As in all other sections of the GED Examination, an unanswered question is considered a wrong answer. Develop the attitude that you must answer every question. Remember that each question carries the same weight. Therefore, you should not spend too much time on any one question. Answer the ones with which you feel most confident and return later to complete the ones you did not initially answer.

Remember that the test is not designed to go from the easiest question to the most difficult. Therefore, it is in your best interest to make every effort to give some attention to each question. The ones near the end of the examination may be the ones that you consider the easiest to answer correctly. If you spend too much time at the questions at the beginning, you will not give justice to those placed near the end.

Remember, if you do not know an answer your next step is to make an educated guess. The more educated the guess, the more choices you have eliminated.

VOCABULARY LIST

AMENDMENT - an addition to an original document.

ANNEX - to acquire territory.

BILL OF RIGHTS - the first ten amendments to the U.S. Constitution, listing the basic rights guaranteed to all citizens.

BUSINESS CYCLE - the changes that occur in an economy ranging from prosperity to depression

CAPITALISM - an economic system that has an emphasis on private ownership and where businesses operate for profit.

CHECKS AND - BALANCES a principle in some governments which holds that the three branches of government should be equal in power.

COMMUNISM - an economic system that seeks to eliminate social classes; the means of production are controlled by the government.

CONCURRENT POWERS - powers, such as the right to tax, belonging to both the central and state governments.

CONFEDERACY - a loose organization.

CONSUMER - one who makes purchases.

CONSTITUTION - the basic foundation of a government.

CULTURAL RELATIVITY a belief that one should judge other cultures by their own standards.

DEMOCRACY - a type of government where the people rule either directly or through their representatives.

DEPRESSION - an extreme downturn in the economy characterized by high unemployment, little or no profit, and few investments.

DIFFUSION - the spreading of ideas, beliefs or traits from one culture to another.

DOMESTIC - relates to events happening within a nation.

ECONOMICS - the study of how people produce, distribute, and consume goods and services.

ETHNOCENTRISM - judging others negatively because they do not conform to ones own standards.

EXECUTIVE - BRANCH the branch of the government that carries out the law.

FEDERAL - GOVERNMENT	another term for a nation's central government
FOREIGN POLICY -	a description of one nation's relationship with other nations.
FREEDMEN -	a term used after the Civil War to describe former slaves.
GEOGRAPHY -	the study of the earth and its physical features, as well as the relationship of life to the physical environment.
GROSS NATIONAL - PRODUCT (GNP)	the total value of an economy's goods and services.
HISTORY -	the study of human's past.
IMPEACH -	to formally accuse a government official of wrongdoing.
IMPERIALISM -	the attempt by a nation to control or dominate a foreign people.
INALIENABLE -	rights that cannot be taken away.
INFLATION -	a decrease in the value of money because too much of it is in circulation.
INTERDEPENDECY-	dependence of two or more things on each other.
INTEGRATION -	providing full rights and membership to all as in racial integration.
INTERSTATE - COMMERCE	trade between two or more states.
INTRASTATE - COMMERCE	trade within a state.
ISOLATIONISM -	a foreign policy stating that it is a nation's best interest not to become involved with other nations in such areas as trade and forming military alliances.
JUDICIAL BRANCH-	the branch of government that interprets the law.
LAISSEZ-FAIRE -	a French term meaning a government's policy of not interfering in the dealings of business.
LEGISLATIVE - BRANCH	the branch of government that makes the law.
MIXED ECONOMY -	a term sometimes used to describe the U.S. economy because its features combine elements of both capitalism and socialism.

NATIONALISM -	concern for the needs of the nation over that of a single state, particular section, or other nations.
NULLIFICATION -	the belief that a state has the right not to follow a law passed by the federal government.
OLIGARCHY -	rule or control by only a few.
POLITICAL SCIENCE -	the study of government.
PRIMARY SOURCE -	an original historical document.
RECESSION -	a moderate slowing of the economy.
SECEDE -	to leave, as when states like Mississippi and Virginia left the Union to join the Confederate States of America.
SECTIONALISM -	more concern for the needs of a section over that of the needs of the nation.
SEGREGATION -	separating groups of people, as in racial segregation.
SEPARATION OF POWERS -	dividing the functions of government (making rules, enforcing rules, interpreting rules) into different sections.
SOCIALISM -	an economic system where the basic industries are owned and operated by the government.
SUFFRAGE -	the right to vote.
TARIFF -	a tax on imported goods.
TOTALITARIANISM -	a system of government where the state has virtually unlimited control over its citizens.
URBANIZATION -	the movement of people to urban (city) areas and the increase of urban areas within a nation.
VETO -	the president's power to reject proposed legislation.
ZERO POPULATION GROWTH (ZPG) -	when the number of births equals the number of deaths.

We will begin our study of social studies by examining some of the important concepts learned from the disciplines that will be covered on the test.

SOCIAL STUDIES/SCIENCE CONCEPTS

Presented below in an outline format are the various social studies/sciences with some of the important concepts that have been learned from these disciplines:

I. History

1. **History is an ongoing process leading to the present.**

    A. Every event, movement, and institution has roots in the past.
    B. People are a product of their past.
    C. Customs, traditions, values, and beliefs are passed from generation to generation.

2. **Historical events have multiple causes and effects**

    A. Though history never repeats itself exactly, similar causes tend to produce similar results.
    B. Historical events may have consequences in times and places other than their own.
    C. Chance and accident influence history which influences ones ability to make predictions.

3. **Change is a constant in history**

    A. The pace of change has varied in different times and places.
    B. In recent times, change has taken place at an accelerated pace.
    C. Factors that can produce change are: inventions and discoveries; changes in the physical environment; the appearance of new ideas, attitudes and values; migration of people.

4. **Change does not necessarily mean progress**

    A. Progress involves change toward a desired goal.
    B. The goals of society vary in different times.
    C. Civilizations develop as people successfully meet problems arising from change; civilizations decline and collapse as people fail to adapt to new circumstances.

II. Geography

1. **Most of man's activities take place on the surface of the earth.**

    A. Where people live influences the way they live.

B. As population density increases, the possibility of conflict and the need for cooperation increase.

2. Earth changes man and man changes earth.

A. Natural occurrences over which man has no control can improve or destroy life and property.

B. People must re-examine their geographic environment in light of changing attitudes, objectives, and technical skills.

3. Geographic factors have a significant role in the life of a nation.

A. No nation is completely self-sufficient.

B. Conflicts between nations often arise because of geographic factors.

4. Maps and globes are visual representatives of the earth or parts of the earth.

A. Map symbols help people read and interpret maps.

B. Scale establishes the relationship between what is seen on a map and the actual size and shape of the area.

III. Political Science

1. Governments exist to make rules for group living.

A. In order to live together, people develop rules and laws.

B. Governments are established to do for the individual what he cannot do for himself.

2. People have developed various forms of government.

A. Governments differ in the way power is obtained and carried out.

B. The nature and structure of governments change.

3. Governments have grown more complex.

A. National and local units of government are interrelated and interdependent.

B. As governments grow more complex, agencies are created to provide additional services.

4. Nations have established international organizations to resolve conflicting interests.

A. Nations establish diplomatic and trade relations with one another.

B. Nations tend to resist giving up their sovereign power.

C. Nations organize with other nations to work together to achieve common aims.

IV. Economics

1. **Human wants are always greater than the available resources.**

   A. Wants are individual and collective.

   B. Wants consist of materials, goods and service.

   C. Scarcity makes it necessary to distribute available resources to best satisfy people's wants.

   D. The conservation of natural resources is necessary for their future availability.

2. **Increased productivity makes possible the greater satisfaction of human's wants.**

   A. Specialization leads to greater interdependence in the economy.

   B. Specialization and the division of labor make possible greater efficiency in producing goods and services.

   C. Increased interdependence brings about increased trade.

3. **Societies develop economic systems in order to distribute limited resources.**

   A. Economic systems (e.g. capitalism, socialism, communism) vary widely in their theory and practice.

   B. Decision-making on how to use limited resources is the basis of every economic system.

4. **Changes in a private enterprise economy result from decisions made by consumers, producers and/or government.**

   A. Prices are basically shaped by the demand for and supply of goods and services.

   B. Producers try to keep their costs of production down and their profits up.

   C. The level of total spending by consumers and the level of investment by businessmen play key roles in influencing recessions and prosperity.

   D. Government policies of taxing, spending, borrowing, and controlling credit and money supplies have powerful effects upon recessions and prosperity.

   E. The economy grows as a result of consumer's decisions to spend and to save and of producers decisions to invest. Government policies also affect this growth.

Study these Social Science concepts to deepen your understanding of these subjects. Use them to help you better comprehend and interpret the questions asked on the GED exam.

Let's try some sample GED Social Studies questions.

1. **Which social scientist would be most concerned with studying interest rates as they affect the degree of consumer spending?**

    (1) historian
    (2) economist
    (3) geographer
    (4) sociologist
    (5) economist

2. **Which of the following is supported by the concepts developed by political scientists?**

    (1) countries are reluctant to sacrifice their own power in settling disputes.
    (2) nations have been developed to offer protection.
    (3) a national government and its local units should cooperate.
    (4) all of the above.
    (5) None of the above.

3. **Which social science would include the most information on the causes of World War II.**

    (1) geography
    (2) history
    (3) anthropology
    (4) sociology
    (5) economics

4. **Which of the following is a false statement?**

    (1) the rate of change for societies is constant
    (2) events can be explained by examining their causes in the past
    (3) a source of change for a society can be ideas from other cultures.
    (4) population density affects group cooperation
    (5) governments have become more complex over time

ANSWERS AND EXPLANATIONS

1. 2 - economist. Interest rates and consumer spending have a great deal of importance in the overall vitality of an economy. While the sociologist and historian might look at such areas, it would be the economist who would be <u>most</u> concerned.

2. 4 - all of the above. Examining the other choices should reveal that they are important findings within this discipline. Therefore, choice 4 would be most correct. Whenever you are sure that at least two of the choices are correct, it is a good decision to go with the all inclusive choice (all of the above).

3. 2 - history. While the other disciplines could offer some information about World War II, it is the subject of history that seeks principally to examine events by studying its causes.

4. 1 - the rate of change for societies is constant. While societies have to respond to changes that might occur, the rate of change is not constant. New ideas, discoveries or other causes of change do not come about at a constant rate. The other statements are true.

Although the history of the United States compared to the history of many nations is not as long, it is nevertheless a complex history. A meaningful approach in reviewing the history of the United States is to examine some of the dominant issues that faced the nation. Certain issues have dominated particular time periods. By understanding the issues you will gain a deeper understanding of this nation's past, present and future.

THE SECOND CONTINENTAL CONGRESS SIGNING THE DECLARATION OF INDEPENDENCE

This section on U.S. history is divided into three units. Each unit will review a major theme by highlighting particular periods in U.S. history. You will note in each unit the themes are explained as conflicts between two opposing forces. This is because there were people, just as there are today, who favored one viewpoint over another viewpoint. The struggles that occurred over the opposing positions were sometimes violent, but all have shaped the course of U.S. history.

I. NATIONALISM vs. SECTIONALISM

Nationalism relates most closely to a feeling or belief that the interests of the entire nation are more important than those of any one section of the nation. The term patriotism is an appropriate synonym for nationalism. Sectionalism suggests that one's primary loyalty is to a particular region of the country.

THE CONSTITUTION OF THE UNITED STATES

Many events question whether the interests of the nation should prevail even though they overshadow a particular section's interests. Two historical examples that will be used to illustrate this issue concern the debate over ratifying the U.S. Constitution and the central cause explaining the outbreak of the American Civil War.

How much power should the central (federal) government possess? This was the key question facing the delegates who met at Philadelphia in 1787. They recognized the government existing under the Articles of Confederation was not meeting the needs of the young nation. The Articles of Confederation provided for no executive branch to carry out the laws. The legislature had no power to tax or control the issuance of money. In addition, amendments to these articles required unanimous approval of the states. The delegates concluded the central government should have more power to lead the nation in areas concerning foreign affairs as well as domestic development.

Although recognizing the above stated need, the U.S. Constitution was a product of many compromises based largely on sectional issues.

Recognizing the need for Southern support, concessions were made to the slavery issue. States were permitted to import slaves until 1808 and for the purposes of representation, five states were to be counted as three non-slave states (3/5 compromise).

There was a concern in the Northeast to protect their new industries. A compromise was made giving Congress the power to place a tariff (tax) on imported goods.

Since the thirteen states ranged widely in their population, concern from both large and small states centered on how each state would be represented in the new central government. If each state had equal representation, as the smaller states favored, the more populated states would not be adequately represented. Likewise, if representation was based solely on population size, the voices of the various smaller states would not be heard. The eventual compromise created two houses for the legislature. One house (the Senate) provided for equal representation from each state while the second (the House of Representatives) based each state's representation on population size.

While the final document formed a basis providing the young nation with a central government possessing the power and authority to lead, it did not resolve the issue of sectionalism. In fact, the central cause of the American Civil War centered on an inability to resolve sectional disputes.

When one thinks about the reason for the Civil War, the focus usually centers on the issue of slavery. Slavery was not only a moral concern, but also involved political and economic differences between the sections. However, the larger concern of which slavery was a part concerned the power of the individual states in relationship to the power of the central government.

The power of the states over the central government was most clearly expressed by John C. Calhoun from South Carolina. Essentially, the belief held that since the individual states entered into a compact in forming the national government, each state could declare a law passed by Congress as unconstitutional. This would make such a law null and void. This doctrine of state's rights also held that a state could end its relationship with the other states by seceding (leaving).

South Carolina tried to carry out this doctrine in response to the Tariff of 1832. The tariff issue was a burning one and later became a factor explaining the outbreak of war. As previously noted, the Northeast favored a high (protective) tariff on imported manufactured goods to protect the industries of this section. The South and to a lesser extent the Western states favored no tariff or a lower one. In response to South Carolina's decree, President Jackson threatened to use federal troops to enforce the law. A compromise bill was proposed and signed into law which lowered the tariff rate the following year. South Carolina withdrew the nullification of the law and made it unnecessary for Jackson to call out the troops.

Immigration was another issue dividing the sections. Both the North and West favored increased immigration, which provided a steady supply of labor for the expanding northern factories and new settlers for the western area. The South opposed large-scale immigration since most new arrivals did not settle there. This factor reduced Southern influence in the central government. In addition, slaves provided the South with a large pool of workers for her plantations.

Territorial expansion also contributed to sectional strife. The North did not favor expansion into the Southwest because it brought the potential of additional slave states into the Union. This did occur as a result of annexing Texas and much of the land received after the Mexican War. Both the South and West favored territorial expansion, which provided additional sources of cheap, fertile land.

Look at the following map and notice the vast areas of land available for expansion after 1850. Notice how from 1845-1850 the southern half of the United States doubled in size. The South felt constrained by the North when it tried to keep it from expanding westward.

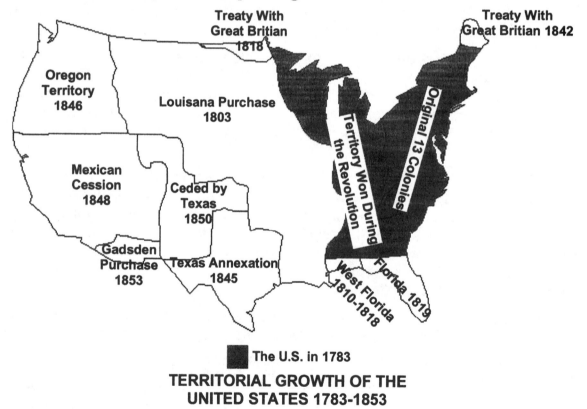

**TERRITORIAL GROWTH OF THE
UNITED STATES 1783-1853**

Examining the causes of the Civil War reveals deep divisions between the sections, particularly the North and South, with the West finding itself more in line with the North. Economic differences, in part, brought about by geographic differences, are a partial explanation. However, the control of the central government became the issue with the South. They concluded that without the strong support of the West they would not have the ability to promote their interests, the South's concern principally being the continuation of slavery and the elimination of the tariff. Finally, a difference existed as to how indivisible was the nation. The Southern viewpoint that states could secede from the Union was bitterly opposed by the North. When giving his primary reason for fighting, Abraham Lincoln stated that above all the war was to preserve the Union.

ABRAHAM LINCOLN

The two historical periods discussed above help illustrate the role played by nationalism and sectionalism in our nation's history.

II. ISOLATION vs. INVOLVEMENT

This unit is concerned with foreign policy. Every nation has a foreign policy even if a nation decides not to become involved with its fellow nation-states.

The dominant question in this unit concerns how involved the United States should be in the affairs of other nations. Reading the newspaper or listening to the news today reveals this is a question still being debated.

The position dominating the early years of U.S. policy was isolationism. It was George Washington who warned the nation to avoid becoming too politically involved with other nations. Being separated by two oceans from Europe and Asia made it easier to honor such advice. Another factor contributing to the general support for isolationism was the vast amount of land that lay westward. Many Americans viewed acquiring this land as their manifest destiny. A look at the map below shows when and how this land was acquired.

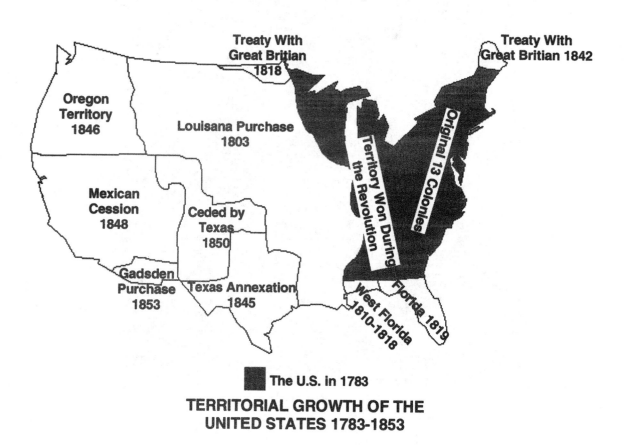

The U.S. in 1783

**TERRITORIAL GROWTH OF THE
UNITED STATES 1783-1853**

While isolationism was the dominant position for the early nineteenth century, there were some notable exceptions to this policy. The War of 1812, fought between the U.S. and Great Britain, has been viewed as the

16

Second American Revolution. The first brought the U.S. political independence from England while the second allowed the U.S. to achieve a greater degree of economic independence.

James Monroe

A second major departure from isolationism occurred in 1823 with the pronouncement of the Monroe Doctrine by President James Monroe. It declared that the Western Hemisphere was closed to further colonization by Europe and further intervention would be viewed as dangerous to America's peace and safety. This rather bold statement by such a young nation was honored in large part because it was supported by England.

By 1890, the American frontier was closed, helping to explain growing U.S. interests abroad. The industrial capacity was at the point of producing a surplus (excess) of goods. Many saw the need to find new markets for these surplus manufactured goods, as well as securing new places to invest and acquire raw materials.

In a bid to join the other world powers in the late nineteenth century, the U.S. developed a policy of imperialism. Attempts to control other nations focused not only on Latin America and the Caribbean, but also areas in the Pacific.

As a result of the Spanish-American War (1898), the U.S. acquired the territories of Puerto Rico, Cuba, Guam and the Philippines. In that same year, the U.S. annexed Hawaii. Further expansion included purchasing the Virgin Islands and acquiring the rights to build a trans-ocean canal in Panama. United States involvement demonstrated her concern for predominance in the affairs of the Western Hemisphere, as well as concern for protecting her commercial interests in the Far East.

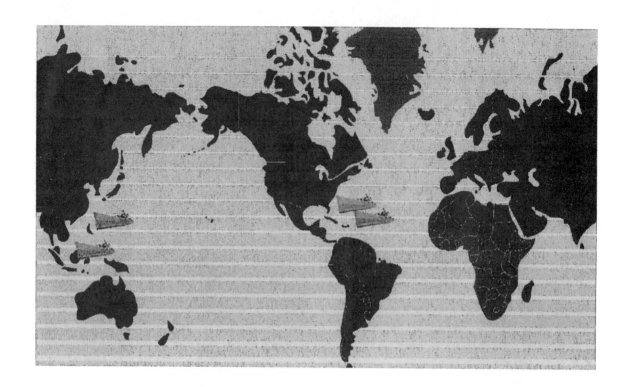

TERRITORY ACQUIRED IN THE SPANISH-AMERICAN WAR

While the U.S. was willing to assume leadership in the Western Hemisphere, the U.S. was neither willing nor prepared to become involved when war broke out in Europe in 1914. The Central Powers of Germany, Austria-Hungary, Turkey and Bulgaria opposed the Allies (Triple Entente) comprised of England, France and Russia (later joined by Italy). The official position declared by President Wilson was one of neutrality, declaring the U.S. would neither favor nor oppose either side.

As the war raged in Europe, the U.S. drew closer to becoming actively involved. Reasons for this were due to many factors, including Germany's use of unrestricted submarine warfare, which caused both the heavy loss of life and property. In addition, U.S. banks and investment firms loaned millions of dollars to the Allies. The Zimmerman Note sent from Germany to Mexico promising the return of Texas, New Mexico, and Arizona, if Mexico would join Germany should the U.S. enter the war helped change the tide of public opinion. In 1917, when Russia pulled out of the war due to the communist revolution, many began to view war as a fight to save democracy. Finally, a feeling prevailed that should the Central Powers win, dictatorial Germany would become the dominant power in Europe, which would perhaps threaten the security of the U.S.

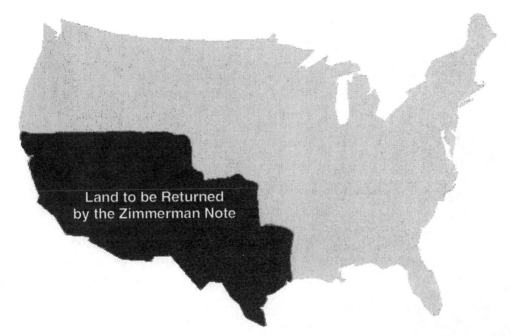

Land to be Returned
by the Zimmerman Note

When President Wilson called for a declaration of war, he asked that this be "the war to end all wars" and that by becoming involved it would help "make the world safe for democracy." The U.S. temporarily abandoned its isolationist stand.

At the conclusion of the war, Wilson hoped to honor his promise by issuing his Fourteen Points. They were designed to end the causes of war. Some of the major points included a call to end secret treaties, to reduce arms, to remove economic barriers on international trade, and to establish a League of Nations to peacefully settle disputes.

Although the European victors were sympathetic to Wilson's view, they were not willing to sacrifice their own national interests. These powers wanted to punish Germany so she would not be able to fight again. Although the Treaty of Versailles, which ended World War I, included provisions for a League of Nations, the treaty's punishment of Germany planted the seeds of discontent for World War II.

U.S. CAPITOL

Under the provisions of the U.S. Constitution, a president is responsible to negotiate treaties, but it is the responsibility of the Senate to ratify (approve) them by a 2/3 vote. When Wilson returned from France, there were many in the Senate who expressed the views of isolationism and were reluctant to ratify the treaty. Their principal objection was Wilson's commitment to join the League of Nations. The Senate feared the U.S. would more likely become involved in another war if it joined. Despite Wilson's pleas, the Senate did not ratify the Treaty of Versailles.

FRANKLIN D. ROOSEVELT

During the years between the two wars (1919-1939) the debate continued to rage between the forces of isolationism and international involvement. By failing to join international organizations like the World Court and League of Nations, as well as passing neutrality legislation, the U.S. attempted to keep out of world affairs. However when war broke out in Europe in 1939, a shift in public opinion did occur. Under orders from President Franklin D. Roosevelt help was provided to England and her allies. After the Japanese attack on Pearl Harbor in Hawaii, the U.S. officially entered the war.

World War II was both a total war involving civilians and armed forces and a global war, where fighting occurred in Europe, Asia, Africa, and across the seven seas. During this war radar, guided missiles, jet-propelled aircrafts, and the atomic bomb were first used.

Following the war, the United States and the Soviet Union emerged as the world's two superpowers. While isolationist sentiment existed, the dominant force since World War II has been one favoring international involvement.

The post World War II struggle between the U.S. and U.S.S.R. is referred to as The Cold War. The struggle includes the political, economic, military, athletic, and scientific areas. While the two nations have not directly fought each other, their influence has been present in such battlegrounds as Korea, Angola, Nicaragua, Afghanistan, and the Middle East.

The relationship of the two superpowers has fluctuated between an easing of tensions (detente) and confrontation. The realities of their respective nuclear arsenals have made them aware of each other's strength.

The question dominating this unit involves to what extent the U.S. should become involved in world affairs. The world of the eighteenth and nineteenth centuries allowed the U.S. to remain isolated from other countries. Today, technology has made communication with even the farthest points almost instantaneous. Places where it once took months to reach now can be reached in hours. These facts, when coupled with the overall strength of the U.S., help explain the direction toward international involvement.

III. LAISSEZ-FAIRE vs. GOVERNMENT INVOLVEMENT

What role should the federal government play in the political, economic, and social lives of Americans? This is the question that will dominate this unit. This question has been and continues to be an area of controversy. Three periods of American history will be reviewed to better understand this theme.

The period after the Civil War (1865-1877) is known as the Reconstruction. The Reconstruction was concerned with the physical rebuilding of the South after four years of war. It was also concerned with the political return of the rebellious states as well as improving the status of the former slaves (freedmen). The main goal was to change the political and social institutions of the South.

MANY PROTEST MARCHES WERE ORGANIZED TO END POLL TAXES AND LITERACY TESTS.

Before the war, slavery was a matter decided by individual states. This was also true in defining a citizen's rights and deciding who could vote. Under the direction of the Radical Republicans, this situation significantly changes. As part of their condition to return to the Union, the states had to accept the 13th Amendment (abolished slavery), 14th Amendment (defined citizenship), and the 15th Amendment (right to vote granted to black males). In the twentieth century, additional amendments and legislation were passed affecting poll taxes, voting age, literacy tests, women's voting rights, and residency requirements to clarify these Reconstruction Amendments.

After the Civil War, and lasting into the early twentieth century, the U.S. began a major transformation from an agricultural based economy to an industrial based economy. During this time, fundamental changes occurred affecting the entire society. They held that individuals, corporations, private charities, and even states have a better idea of how to conduct their affairs than the federal government. Large corporations dominated the economy. Railroad mileage increased from 3,000 to 200,000 miles. Electricity and petroleum became new sources of power. Technological innovations like the telephone, phonograph, electric light bulb, airplane, and radio were invented. Factories became a major place of employment. Immigration increased but this time from Asia, Southern Europe, and Eastern Europe as these people sought better political and economic conditions in the U.S.

RAILROAD MILEAGE EXPLODED AFTER THE CIVIL WAR

These changes brought an increased standard of living for many Americans and created opportunities that did not previously exist. However, industrialization and urbanization created problems for which there were no easy solutions. Working conditions were often dangerous and many people worked long hours for low pay. Some corporations tried to find ways of eliminating all forms of competition. Living conditions were often inadequate and unsanitary. Children were often exploited in the workplace. The small farmer saw his economic power erode. Political power rested in the hands of the wealthy. Finally, the new immigrants (blacks and women) were often victims of discrimination.

GIRL BEING EXPLOITED WORKING IN A BOX FACTORY

Workers, farmers, and groups supporting other affected peoples sought help from the federal government as a means of improving their condition. The traditional role of the federal government (and to a lesser extent the state and local governments) was to adopt a laissez-faire (hands-off) policy. However, by the late nineteenth and early twentieth centuries, reformers sought to correct many of the ills through political means.

Curbs were passed to regulate the size of big businesses, as well as the rate certain industries could change. Legislation affecting meat inspection and other foods was enacted. Factory and building codes were adopted. Compulsory education laws for children were passed in many states. Many cities and states allowed citizens the powers of recall (removal of government officials), initiative (introduce laws), and referendum (vote on laws). Amendments to the Constitution were passed which provided for a graduated income tax, the election of Senators by citizens rather than the state legislatures and the right of women to vote. These changes set the stage for greater involvement by government in the political, economic, and social lives of Americans later in this century.

The debate over the extent of government involvement was raised to new heights during the Great Depression of the 1930's. The depression was triggered by the stock market crash in October of 1929. However, the underlying causes were many and could be found throughout much of the

1920's. Among the major causes were banks making unsafe loans, wild speculation in real estate and the stock markets, uneven distribution of wealth, low income among farmers, and a high protective tariff that caused a decline in international trade. In addition, American industries overexpanded their production while many consumers lacked the income to purchase the goods.

BREAD LINES EXPLODED DURING THE DEPRESSION

The depression affected the entire nation and was part of a general one that existed throughout the world. In the U.S., over 5,000 banks closed leaving many depositors penniless. The unemployment rate reached 25% while a significant number of people were underemployed (those who took jobs in which they were overqualified). The average income per person declined from $857 in 1929 to $590 in 1933. The GNP (gross national product - total value of all goods and services) dropped from $104 to $74 billion during these same years.

By examining the chart on the next page you can see the downward spiral effect of a depression.

THE DOWNWARD SPIRAL OF DEPRESSION

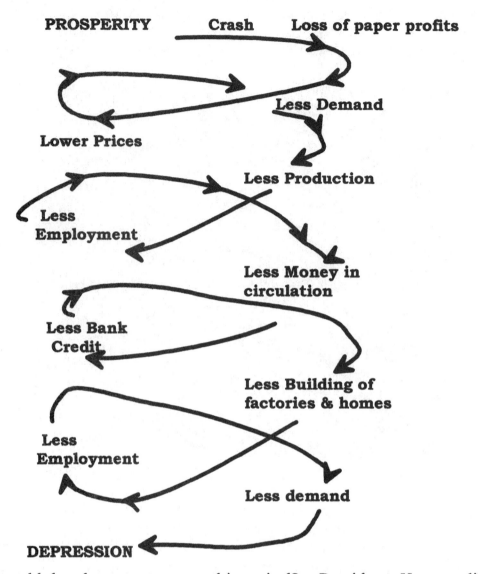

PROSPERITY   Crash   Loss of paper profits

Less Demand

Lower Prices

Less Production

Less Employment

Less Money in circulation

Less Bank Credit

Less Building of factories & homes

Less Employment

Less demand

DEPRESSION

What could be done to reverse this spiral? President Hoover, like his Republican predecessors (Harding and Coolidge) believed in the laissez-faire philosophy. In addition, none of them saw the signals of the coming depression. When it arrived Hoover did not believe that the federal government had the power or responsibility to do very much.

President Franklin D. Roosevelt, a Democrat, took office in 1933 holding a different viewpoint on the role of the federal government. His program to end the Depression was called the New Deal. It contained three broad goals: **a.** relief (direct aid to the needy); **b.** recovery (stimulate the economy); and **c.** reform (replace the factors that led to the depression). Relief programs included giving part-time employment to students and giving money to states for direct relief to feed and clothe the needy. Recovery included giving workers the right to organize, paying farmers to limit their crops, lending money to help homeowners keep their homes, and establishing agreements with other nations to improve international trade. Finally, reform programs included government regulation of the stock market, support of collective bargaining between employer and union, establishing a minimum wage, insurance on bank deposits and social security for the aged, disabled and unemployed. Many of the New Deal programs were controversial, but they established a direction of government intervention that lasts to the present.

THE NEW DEAL INCLUDED MANY LARGE PROJECTS TO PUT PEOPLE TO WORK. THIS DAM FOR THE TENNESSEE VALLEY AUTHORITY IS A GOOD EXAMPLE.

The role and scope of government has changed since our nation's beginnings. However, those who favor less intervention continue to make their voices heard. They hold individuals, corporations, private charities and even states have a better idea of how to conduct their affairs than the federal government.

Following are a series of questions dealing with U.S. history. The questions will measure your understanding of the material beyond the simple recall of facts. Instead, you will be asked to analyze and interpret the material in order to make logical conclusions. The questions in this section, as well as the other sections, are the types you will find on your GED examination.

Items 1 and 2 refer to the map below:

**TERRITORIAL GROWTH OF THE
UNITED STATES 1783-1853**

1. **The United States approximately doubled its size by the**

   1) land gained from the Mexican War in 1848
   2) various treaties with Great Britain
   3) Louisiana Purchase
   4) annexation of Texas
   5) gaining Florida in 1819

2. **United States expansion from the Atlantic to the Pacific ocean was due to:**

   1) purchase
   2) war
   3) treaty negotiations
   4) none of the above
   5) all of the above

3. **Which of the following was <u>not</u> a result of U.S. industrialization?**

1) the growth of cities
2) a decrease in the quantity of goods
3) a higher standard of living
4) the establishment of new industries
5) an increase in pollution

4. **Which would be consistent with one of Wilson's Fourteen Points?**

1) an increase in the tariff rates to keep out Japanese goods
2) a secret military alliance between the Soviet Union and Iran
3) a settlement of territorial disputes by the United Nations
4) an increase in world-wide defense spending
5) the break-up of Germany into five separate countries

5. **Which of the following is the most correct statement concerning U.S. expansion?**

1) expansion has played a significant part in American history
2) all expansion resulted from military action against a European nation
3) expansion first took place after the Spanish-American War
4) expansion stopped after the closing of the West
5) expansion was always done unfairly

Item 6 refers to the excerpt below taken from President Wilson's 1917 War Message:

Property can be paid for; the lives of peaceful and innocent people cannot be.... We will not choose the path of submission and suffer the most sacred rights of our Nation and our people to be ignored or violated.

We are glad, now that we see the facts with no veil of false pretense about them, to fight thus for the ultimate peace of the world and for the liberation of its peoples, the German peoples included: for the rights of nations great and small and the privilege of men every-where to choose their way of life and of obedience. The world must be made safe for democracy. Its peace must be planted upon the tested foundations of political liberty.... We desire no conquest, no dominion. We seek no indemnities for ourselves, no material compensation for the sacrifices we shall freely make.

6. **In asking Congress for a declaration of war, Wilson emphasized the need for the U.S. to:**

1) punish Germany
2) advance the cause of liberty
3) gain territory
4) protect its investments
5) get redress for an insult

Items 7, 8 and 9 refer to the passage below from an American author of the early twentieth century.

> "Cut up by the two-thousand-revolutions-a-minute flyers, and mixed with half a ton of other meat, no odor that ever was in a ham could make any difference.... there would come all the way back from Europe old sausage that had been rejected, and that was moldy and white-it would dosed with borax and glycerine, and dumped into the hoppers, and made over again for home consumption.
>
> There would be meat that had tumbled out on the floor, in the dirt and sawdust, where the workers had trampled and spit uncounted germs. There would be meat stored in great piles in the rooms; and the water from leaky roofs would drip over it, and thousands of rats would race about on it.
>
> These rats were nuisances, and the packers would put poisoned bread out for them; they would die and then rats, bread and meat would go into the hoppers together—and the man who did the shoveling would not trouble to lift out a rat even when he saw one....
>
> Under the system of rigid economy, which the packers enforced, there were some jobs that it only paid to do once in a long time, and among these was the cleaning-out of the waste barrels. Every spring they did it; and cart load after cart load of it would be taken up and dumped into the hoppers with fresh meat and sent out to the public's breakfast....

from Upton Sinclair's "The Jungle"

7. **The title that best expresses the idea of the reading is:**

1) "A Cost-Effective Way to Prepare Sausage"
2) "Preventing Waste in the Meat Packing Industry"
3) "Sausage May Be Hazardous to Your Health"
4) "How to Make Sausage"
5) "Spring Cleaning"

8. **The author's major complaint concerning the meat packing plants was they were:**

   1) old
   2) inefficient
   3) unlighted
   4) producing sausage that tasted bad
   5) unsanitary

9. **From this passage, it can be inferred that the author would most favor:**

   1) labor unions
   2) more modern machinery
   3) emphasis on plant control of rats
   4) government regulation of this industry
   5) shorter workdays

Items 10, 11, and 12 refer to the three graphs below that represent different ways a society could develop.

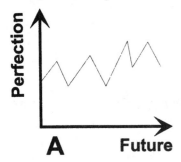 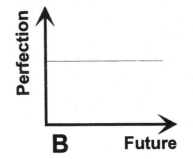 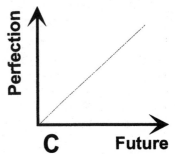

10. **Which graph or graphs represent a society that is moving in a cycle (periods of progress followed by decay, progress, decay, etc.)?**

    1) A
    2) B
    3) C
    4) A and C
    5) A, B, and C

11. **Which graph or graphs represent a society that is making constant progress toward perfection?**

    1) A
    2) B
    3) C
    4) A and C
    5) A, B, and C

12. **Which graph represents a society that is static (remains the same)?**

1) A
2) B
3) C
4) A and C
5) A, B, and C

13. **In the government provided by the Articles of Confederation:**

1) the states were the final authority
2) Congress enforced its will by its power of taxation
3) the central government exercised most of the power
4) consent of a majority of states was necessary for amending the Articles
5) England had to be consulted on all major decisions

14. **When the Constitutional Convention accepted a compromise on the form of the new legislature, it resolved a conflict between:**

1) North and South
2) the two largest states
3) slaveholders and abolitionists
4) the large and small states
5) imports and exports

15. **The question of whether a state may secede from the Union was answered in the negative by:**

1) state's rights theory
2) The Reconstruction
3) the Civil War
4) the War of 1812
5) the Louisiana Purchase

16. **Sectionalism:**

1) still exists because of different economic and political issues
2) disappeared after the Civil War
3) was favored only by the South
4) was resolved when Alaska became a state
5) only involved the issue of slavery

17. **A protective tariff is intended to protect the:**

    1) consumer from high prices on imported goods
    2) consumer on goods produced within the country
    3) manufacturer from lower prices on goods imported into the country
    4) manufacturer from higher prices on raw materials produced within the country
    5) the budget for the military by guaranteeing that there will be enough money to pay the soldiers

Item 18 is based on the excerpt from the Declaration of Independence (1776):

We hold these truths to be self-evident; that all men are created equal; that they are endowed by their Creator with inherent and inalienable rights; that among these are life, liberty, and the pursuit of happiness; that to secure these rights, governments are instituted among men, deriving their just powers from the consent of the governed; that whenever any form of government becomes destructive of these ends, it is the right of the people to alter or to abolish it, and to institute new government, laying its foundation on such principles, and organizing its powers in such form as to them shall seem most likely to effect safety and happiness.

18. **What did Thomas Jefferson, the author of this document believe should be the aim of government?**

    1) to prevent revolution
    2) to improve one's relationship with the creator
    3) to protect people from outsiders
    4) to foster power
    5) to assure that citizens have their natural rights

19. **Which is the least biased description of the presidency of Franklin D. Roosevelt?**

    1) Mr. Roosevelt was an outstanding president.
    2) Mr. Roosevelt increased government involvement through his New Deal program.
    3) Mr. Roosevelt had difficulty making decisions.
    4) Mr. Roosevelt failed in his efforts to get the nation out of the Great Depression.
    5) Without the actions taken by Mr. Roosevelt the depression would have lasted five more years.

I must make two honest confessions to you, my Christian and Jewish brothers. First, I must confess that over the past few years I have been gravely disappointed with the white moderates. I have almost reached the regrettable conclusions that the Negro's great stumbling in his stride toward freedom is not the White Citizens Councils or the Ku Klux Klanner, but the White moderate, who is more devoted to "order" than to justice; who prefers a negative peace which is the absence of tensions to a positive peace which is the presence of justice; who constantly says: "I agree with you in the goal you seek, but I cannot agree with your methods of direct action; who paternalistically believes he can set the time-table for another man's freedom; who lives by a mythical concept of time and who constantly advises the Negro to wait for more convenient reason." Shallow understanding from people of good will is more frustrating than absolute misunderstanding from people of ill will. Lukewarm acceptance is much more bewildering than outright rejection.

(King, Jr., Martin Luther. <u>Why We Can't Wait</u>)

20. **Martin Luther King's purpose in writing this passage was to:**

1) condemn the South
2) start a revolution in the U.S.
3) change the attitude of many moderate white Americans
4) to thank white America
5) to explain why the time has not yet come for change

Item 21 refers to the cartoon below:

"WE ARE WINNING THE WAR"

21. **Which of the following best expresses the intentions of the cartoonist?**

1) to show how much taller Lyndon Johnson was than Ho Chi Minh
2) the cartoonist is stressing that essentially everybody sees the same thing
3) the cartoonist's main purpose is to show how Americans have more modern means of mass communication
4) the cartoonist is stating that each side presents its own particular view to its people
5) the cartoonist wants to show that Ho Chi Minh is as good a statesman as Lyndon Johnson

Items 22 and 23 are based on the tables below.

Year	Millions Employed	Millions Unemployed
1929	47.6	1.5
1930	45.5	4.3
1931	42.4	8.0
1932	38.9	12.1
1933	38.7	12.8
1934	40.9	11.3
1935	42.2	10.6
1936	44.4	9.0
1937	46.3	7.7
1938	44.2	10.3
1939	45.7	9.4
1940	47.5	8.1

Bank Assets

Year	Billions of Dollars
1929	72.3
1930	74.2
1931	70.0
1932	57.2
1933	51.3
1934	55.9
1935	59.9
1936	66.8
1937	68.4
1938	67.7
1939	73.1
1940	79.7

Number of Factories

Year	Number
1929	206,663
1931	171,450
1933	139,325
1935	167,916
1937	166,794
1939	173,802

Consumer Expenditures

Year	Billions of Dollars
1929	78.9
1930	70.9
1931	61.3
1932	49.3
1933	46.3
1934	51.8
1935	56.2
1936	62.6
1937	67.2
1938	64.6
1939	67.5
1940	71.8

22. **The worst year of the Great Depression was:**

1) 1929
2) 1932
3) 1933
4) 1938
5) 1940

23. **Which of the following is supported by the data?**

1) the New Deal programs brought a quick end to the depression
2) bank assets did not return to the pre-depression figures until after 1940
3) there was a steady growth in the economy after 1933
4) as consumers spent more the assets of the banks increased
5) unemployment doubled from 1930-1932

Items 24-26 refer to the excerpts below:

A. "The President is the direct representative of the American people; he possesses original executive powers and absorbs in himself all executive functions and responsibilities; and it is his especial duty to protect the liberties and rights of the people and the integrity of the Constitution against the Senate or the House of Representatives, or both together."

B. "I have never felt that it was my duty to attempt to coerce Senators or Representatives.... It seems to me public administrators would get along better if they would restrain the impulse to butt in or be dragged into trouble. They should remain silent until an issue is reduced to its lowest...."

C. "It became necessary for me to choose whether, using only the existing means, agencies, and processes which Congress had provided, I should let the Government fall at once into ruin or whether, availing myself of the broader powers conferred by the Constitution in cases of insurrection, I would make an effort to save it, with all its blessings, for the present age and for posterity."

D. "The President can never again be the mere domestic figure he has been throughout so large a part of our history. The nation has risen to the first rank in power and resources.... Our President must always, henceforth, be one of the great powers of the world, whether he acts greatly or wisely or not.... He must stand always at the front of our affairs, and the office will be as big and as influential as the man who occupies it."

24. Which viewpoint was most likely expressed by Abraham Lincoln?

 1) A
 2) B
 3) C
 4) D
 5) None of the passages

25. Which viewpoint shows a concern for U.S. involvement in world affairs?

 1) A
 2) B
 3) C
 4) D
 5) None of the passages

26. **Which viewpoint suggests a limited view of presidential power?**

   1) A
   2) B
   3) C
   4) D
   5) All of the passages

Items 27 and 28 refer to the table below:

SLAVE POPULATION OF THE UNITED STATES, 1790-1860			
YEAR	NORTHEAST	NORTH CENTRAL	SOUTH
1790	40,354	——	657,327
1800	36,370	135	857,097
1810	27,081	3,304	1,160,977
1820	18,001	11,329	1,508,977
1830	2,780	25,879	1,980,384
1840	765	56,604	2,427,986
1850	236	87,422	3,116,629
1860	18	114,948	3,838,765

27. **Which section consistently had the greatest number of slaves?**

   1) Northeast
   2) North Central
   3) South
   4) West
   5) South and West

28. **Which of the following is not supported by the table?**

   1) Slavery was a dying institution by 1860
   2) the South had the most to lose by the end of slavery
   3) slaves were not needed for the Northern factories
   4) the North Central states experienced a growth in slaves from 1800-1860
   5) There were no slaves in the North in 1860

1. (3) Louisiana Purchase. Look at the dates to assist you in making the size comparison.

2. (5) All of the above. From the map you can see that the U.S. expanded through purchases, war with Mexico and treaty negotiations with Great Britain.

3. (2) Decreases in the quantity of goods. Industrialization brought a mass production of goods. The other three choices were results of industrialization.

4. (3) United Nations. The U. N. was an outgrowth of Wilson's idea for a League of Nations. The other choices could be seen as causes for war which is something Wilson hoped to avoid through his Fourteen Points.

5. (1) Expansion has played a significant part in American history. You must think of expansion in a broad sense to include the entire history of the U.S. Look at the map that helped you with questions 1 and 2.

6. (2) Advance the cause of liberty. Wilson believed that the entry of the U.S. would help make the world safe for democracy.

7. (3) "Sausage May Be Hazardous to Your Health." One of Sinclair's purposes was to show the horrible conditions of the meat packing industry. His book contributed to the passage of the Meat Inspection Act of 1906. The other choices suggest that methods used were acceptable.

8. (5) Unsanitary. Each of the four paragraphs provides at least one example of the unsanitary conditions.

9. (4) Government regulation of this industry. Sinclair favors the position of some outside force watching over this industry. Modern machinery and rat control would only deal with some of the problems. Labor unions might improve working conditions, but would not necessarily affect the quality of the production.

10. (1)

11. (3)

12. (2) Examine the direction of the line in each graph to see its direction in comparison to the future axis and the perfection axis.

13. (1)   The states were the final authority. The term confederation suggests a loosely bound group. Choices 2 and 3 suggest the central government was dominant over the states, which was not true. Choice 4 is not accurate because an amendment to the Articles required unanimous approval.

14. (4)   The large and small states. The concern in devising a legislature was not to slight either the small or large states. Hence, two houses were developed.

15. (3)   Civil War. The key word in the question is "negative." Lincoln initially fought the war to preserve the Union in response to secession.

16. (1)   Still exists because of different economic and political issues. Sectionalism continues because there are issues that affect sections differently (e.g. domestic oil prices).

17. (3)   Manufacturer from lower prices on goods imported into the country. A tariff is a tax on imports.

18. (5)   To assure that citizens have their natural rights. Jefferson states that government exists for the people, not the rulers, and that people must be served.

19. (2)   Mr. Roosevelt increased government through his New Deal Program. The answer does indicate a particular viewpoint, unlike the other choices.

20. (3)   Change the attitude of many moderate white Americans. The theme is King's concern over indecision of the moderate whites.

21. (4)   The cartoonist is stating that each side presents its own particular view to its people. Despite the destruction of the Vietnam War, the leaders of both countries kept trying to convince their respective citizens that they were winning. This choice is more compelling than Choice 2, which suggests that people see what they want to see. These leaders desire to communicate their message to others.

22. (3)   Compare the figures for each of the four charts.

23. (4)   As consumers spent more, the assets of the banks increased. Compare the figures from these two tables.

24. (3)   The key word is "insurrection"; it also states the intention to save the Constitution by not letting the government fall.

25. (4)   Examine the references indicating the need to be a "first rank power" and "be one of the great powers of the world". Woodrow Wilson made this statement.

26. (2)   Most presidents of the twentieth century have viewed their office as powerful. One way of demonstrating this power has been to influence

Congress in the passing of legislation. This statement was made by Calvin Coolidge.

27. (3) South. Compare the figures for the three sections over the period from 1790-1860.

28. (1) Slavery was a dying institution by 1860. The number of slaves in the South actually reached a new high in 1860. The other choices are supported by the figures.

In this section you will read about the government of the U.S. with special attention given to the U.S. Constitution. The questions at the end will measure your understanding of the material presented, as well as your ability to correctly reason answers from the diagrams and charts provided.

The U.S. Constitution forms the legal foundation of the national, state, and local governments. All laws of these governments must be consistent with this document. The government established under the U.S. Constitution created a government based on law and not of men.

THE U.S. CONSTITUTION

This document was founded upon certain basic principles reflecting the concerns of many leading European thinkers, as well as the various delegates to the Constitutional Convention in 1787. One important issue was the delegation of power. All governments, regardless of their level or type, have the primary functions or powers. They make laws (legislate), carry out the laws (execute), and interpret the laws (judiciate). If all of these functions rest in one person or group of persons, the result is often tyranny. The founding fathers created a separation of powers in the hope that the government would be more responsible and free. The first three articles to the Constitution outline the qualifications, responsibilities, and powers of the legislative branch (Congress), executive branch (President), and judicial branch (Supreme Court).

In addition to separating the powers into three branches, the Constitution also provided for a system of checks and balances. The idea behind this is to give each branch the responsibility of performing their own duties while having the power to "check" the power of the other two branches.

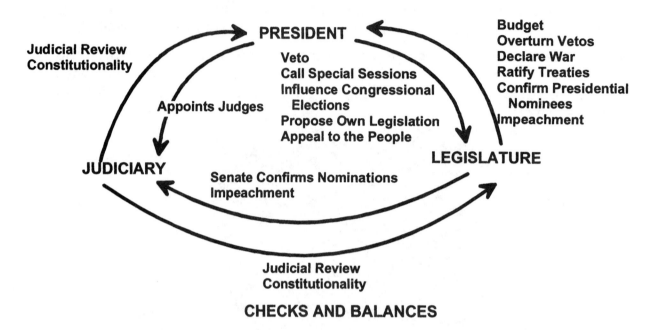

CHECKS AND BALANCES

The President checks the judiciary by being able to appoint all federal judges. Since judges may serve for life, the President's ability to appoint them can help the courts to reflect his political beliefs for many years after he has left office. However, a President may not interfere with judges who are hearing a case and judges never conference with a President before making their decisions.

The President can check the legislative branch through the power of the veto, which stops a bill from becoming law. Under the Constitution, a President can call both houses into special session in order to meet needs or solve problems. Other checks not specifically granted by the Constitution but developed over time: are influencing congressional elections through personal campaigning, proposing his own legislation to Congress, and appealing directly to the people for support.

Congress has powers serving as checks over the judicial branch. While the President nominates people to serve as federal judges, it falls upon the Senate to approve or reject such nominations. In addition, Congress has the authority to impeach (formally accuse) and remove a judge from office for any conduct violating the public's trust.

Since it is the responsibility of Congress to establish a budget for the executive branch (the power of the purse), a powerful check is held over the President. Even a presidential veto is not final because it may be overturned by a two-thirds vote of Congress. The legislative branch also has the power to declare war, establish limits for foreign aid, and effect the size of the military, while the Senate has the authority to ratify treaties. In addition, the Senate confirms presidential appointments like Cabinet members and ambassadors. Finally, this branch has the right to impeach and remove members of the executive branch including the President.

Through its power of judicial review the courts can check both the legislative and executive branches. Judicial review gives the courts the power to examine laws and executive decisions. Any federal court can declare such actions as unconstitutional after someone challenges them in court. If a law has been declared as unconstitutional, it ceases to have any legal force. Such cases usually involve the various levels of the court system with the final decision resting in the Supreme Court.

In addition to the principles of government discussed above, the Constitution also provides for a federal system of government. This means power is divided between the central and state governments with some power belonging solely to either and some being shared (concurrent powers). Among the powers reserved for the federal government (central government) are the powers to declare war, make treaties, and regulate interstate affairs. Reserved powers for the fifty state governments include the right to control local firearms, schools, and marriages. In addition, they regulate the conduct of business within their borders (intrastate) and ratify amendments. Among those powers considered to be concurrent are the powers to tax, establish a court system, and conduct elections.

The U.S. Constitution is the oldest written national constitution in the world. Although the U.S. has experienced significant changes over the past 200 years, the document remains intact. A major reason why it still exists is because the delegates anticipated future change. The language used was often general, leaving to future generations the task of adapting the document to meet new problems and changing circumstances. Many of these interpretations have led to increased federal authority in many areas of American life. Congress has used its implied powers to bring about these changes.

Another reason that explains why the Constitution has remained flexible over the years is the amending process. Each amendment assumes the same authority as the original Constitution. The first ten amendments are better known as the Bill of Rights. They were adopted immediately after the Constitution's ratification. The Bill of Rights was designed to protect individual citizens from abuses by government. Among the freedoms granted are speech, religion, assembly, and press. The other amendments since 1791 include four broad categories. Civil rights amendments, such as abolishing slavery, were written to protect the rights of individuals abused or denied by existing practices. Some amendments have involved voting procedure and the process of how elections are conducted. The last amendment (the 26th), granting eighteen-year olds the right to vote, belongs under this category. Amendments have been passed affecting terms of office and succession to office. Finally, amendments such as the establishment of an income tax have been ratified because (without an amendment) they may have been considered unconstitutional.

An important feature of the U.S. government (not provided for by the Constitution) is the use of political parties. In a democracy, political parties are viewed as necessary organizations to bring people of similar beliefs together for the purpose of translating those beliefs into law. Parties involve citizens in politics by promoting programs and attacking others. They provide choices, make election to office possible, and supply people to run the government.

THE TWO PARTY SYSTEM MEANS ONE CANDIDATE ALMOST ALWAYS GETS A MAJORITY. NOT ALWAYS THE ONE PREDICTED BY THE POLLS.

Almost all nations of the world have political parties, but some like the People's Republic of China outlaw all political parties but one. Several democratic nations have three or more well-organized parties, but often find it difficult to form a clear-cut majority. In the American political system a two party system has developed which has made it easier to form a majority and provide stability. Although third (minor) parties have existed throughout U.S. history, their primary purpose has been not to actually win elections, but influence public opinion in the hope of one day having their views accepted by a majority of people.

A more recent tradition (not included in the Constitution) is the growth of independent agencies. They have been called the "fourth branch" of the federal government. These agencies regulate the actions of companies involved in interstate affairs. Regulatory commissions like the Federal Communication Commission affect radio and television broadcasting by setting standards. This commission also is concerned with telephone communication. The Civil Aeronautics Board sets airline rates and approves routes. Other agencies like the Federal Trade Commission (FTC) try to eliminate unfair trade practices while the Securities and Exchange Commission requires full disclosure of all financial information by a company selling stocks and bonds.

Use the previous pages to help you answer the questions on the following pages.

SAMPLE GED QUESTIONS - AMERICAN GOVERNMENT

1. **Political parties are needed in a democracy in order to:**
   - (1) organize a political majority
   - (2) educate citizens about the issues of the day
   - (3) provide candidates with a means to run for office
   - (4) Help candidates spread their views
   - (5) all of these

2. **In a democracy like the U.S., the wishes of the majority must always outweigh the wishes of a minority. This statement is:**
   - (1) true
   - (2) false; the minority must always come first
   - (3) false; certain basic rights should be safe-guarded
   - (4) false; the minority is encouraged to leave
   - (5) true; in a democracy there is no room for dissent

3. **All of the following are rights guaranteed to each American except:**
   - (1) freedom of speech
   - (2) the right to assemble
   - (3) right to a guaranteed annual income
   - (4) freedom of religion
   - (5) freedom from discrimination

Item 4 refers to the diagram below:

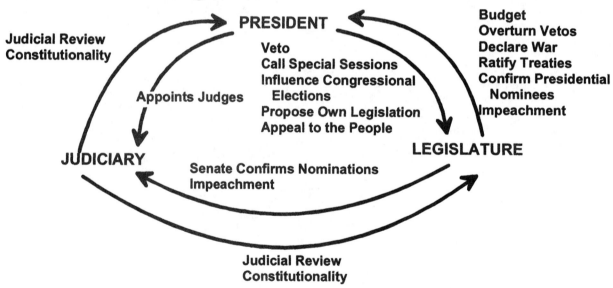

48

4. Which of the following is a check the executive branch has over the legislative branch?

       (1)   ability to override a veto
       (2)   appoint members to Congress
       (3)   declare laws unconstitutional
       (4)   veto a law
       (5)   appoints judges

Item 5 refers to the passage below:

"But the great security against a gradual concentration of the several powers in the same department consists in giving to those who administer each department the necessary constitutional means and personal motives to resist encroachments of the others. The provision for defense must in this, as in all other cases, be made commensurate to the danger of attack.

    <u>Ambition must be made to counteract ambition.</u>

The interest of the man must be connected with the constitutional rights of the place. It may be a reflection on human nature, that such devices should be necessary to control the abuses of government. But what is government itself, but the greatest of all reflections on human nature? If men were angels, no government would be necessary. If angels were to govern men, neither external nor internal controls on government would be necessary. In framing a government which is to be administered by men over men, the great difficulty lies in this: you must first enable the government to control the governed; and in the next place oblige it to control itself."

(From <u>The Federalist</u>, No. 51 by James Madison)

5. Which idea would the author support?

       (1)   checks and balances
       (2)   dictatorship
       (3)   anarchy (the absence of government)
       (4)   oligarchy (rule by religious organizations)
       (5)   all of the above

Item 6 refers to the quote below:

"Power corrupts. Absolute power corrupts absolutely."
- Lord Acton

6. **The founding fathers show their agreement with this quote by providing in the Constitution:**

    (1)   political parties
    (2)   an amendment process
    (3)   state governments
    (4)   a system of checks and balances
    (5)   freedom of speech

7. **Federal aid to schools is welcomed by some people in the various state governments, but others fear that federal money also means that the federal government will:**

    (1)   impose higher property taxes
    (2)   build bigger schools
    (3)   eliminate jobs
    (4)   force the schools to teach religious subjects
    (5)   gain greater control of school curriculum and policy

Item 8 refers to the chart below:

PARTY	DATES	DESCRIPTION
LIBERTY PARTY	1840-48	First anti-slavery party
FREE-SOIL PARTY	1848-56	Favored free territory in the West
AMERICAN PARTY (KNOW-NOTHING)	1852-60	Anti-immigrant, anti-Catholic Nickname grew out of members claim, when questioned, "to know nothing" about the party.
PROHIBITION PARTY	1869-	Based on opposition to use of alcohol. Worked for passage of the 18th amendment.
GREENBACK PARTY	1876-84	Supported paper money, entension of federal power, and the income tax.
SOCIALIST PARTY	1890-	Favors government ownership of natural resources and major industries.
POPULIST PARTY	1891-96	Farmer and worker party; anti-monopoly
PROGRESSIVE PARTY	1924-46	LaFollette's semi-socialist party; promoted government ownership and regulation of business and resources.
AMERICAN INDEPENDENT PARTY	1968-	George Wallaces's states rights party.
PEACE AND FREEDOM PARTY	1968-	Anti-war, anti-draft, leftwing movement.

8. **Which of the following is <u>not</u> a conclusion that can be drawn from the chart above?**

   (1)   third parties have served no purpose in U.S. history
   (2)   many third parties last for only a short duration
   (3)   third parties tend to focus on specific issue
   (4)   third parties can be found in the 19th and 20th centuries
   (5)   third parties are only concerned with finances

Items 9 and 10 refer to the excerpts from a presidential speech:

But here is the challenge to democracy: In this I see tens of millions of its citizens - a substantial part of its whole population - who at this very moment are denied the greater part of what the very lowest standards of today call the necessities of life.

I see millions where daily lives in the city and on the farm continue under conditions labeled indecent by a so-called polite society half a century ago.

I see millions denied education, recreation and the opportunity to better their lot and the lot of their children.

I see millions lacking the means to buy the products of farms and factories and by their poverty, denying work and productiveness to many other millions.

I see one third of a nation ill-housed, ill-clad, ill-nourished.

(From F.D. Roosevelt, <u>First</u> <u>Inaugural</u> <u>Address</u>)

9. **What is FDR referring to in this passage?**

     (1)   World War II
     (2)   the weakness of the Constitution
     (3)   the Great Depression
     (4)   the failure of democracy
     (5)   Germany after World War II

10. **What idea below would FDR support?**

     (1)   greater involvement by the federal government
     (2)   less involvement by the federal government
     (3)   no involvement by the federal government
     (4)   abolish the government
     (5)   send the poor to another country

Below are quotations from the U.S. Constitution. These are followed by newspaper headlines. For each of the headlines select the quotation from the Constitution which applies to that headline.

- A. "The right of the people to be secure in their persons, houses, papers...against unreasonable searches...shall not be violated..." (Amendment IV)

- B. "...no person shall be...compelled in any criminal case to be a witness against himself...." (Amendment V)

- C. "...the accused shall...have...the assistance of counsel for his defense." (Amendment VI)

- D. "...nor cruel and unusual punishments inflicted." (Amendment VIII)

- E. "...nor shall any state deprive...any person within its jurisdiction the equal protection of the laws." (Amendment XIV)

11. State Refuses To Integrate Schools

  (1) A
  (2) B
  (3) C
  (4) D
  (5) E

12. Narcotics Suspect Charges Police Illegally Searched His Apartment

  (1) A
  (2) B
  (3) C
  (4) D
  (5) E

13. Group Protests Death Penalty

  (1) A
  (2) B
  (3) C
  (4) D
  (5) E

Items 14 and 15 refer to the chart below:

| Bill proposed by a Congressperson | → | Bill is assigned to a committee in accordance with its topic.

House has 21 committees.
Senate has 17 committees. |

Full committee acts on the bill.
It may decide:
1. Bill is not needed.
2. Bill should be revised.
3. Approve the bill and send it to the floor.
4. Send it to the floor without approval.

← A committee sub-committee holds public hearings on major bills.

Sub-committee reports back recommendations to the full committee.

Report bill to the full chamber (House of Senate) for debate and vote.

House has limited debate.
Senate has no limit on debate.

→ If approved the bill goes to the other chamber.

1. May have a similar bill of its own.
2. Send the bill to a committee.
3. Vote and aprove the bill as it stands.

Both chambers iron out differences in bills in conference.

BILL IS LAW ← Send final bill to the President.
He may:
1. Sign it.
2. Veto it.
(Both chambers with a 2/3 vote can override a veto.)

14. For a bill to become a law it <u>must</u> be

     (1)   approved by both houses of Congress
     (2)   signed by the president
     (3)   debated by the Supreme Court
     (4)   approved by a committee
     (5)   approved by one house of Congress

15. Which conclusion can be drawn from the chart?

     (1)   the two houses do not usually confer with each other
     (2)   much work is done by the committees
     (3)   the House and Senate can ask the President to sign different versions of a bill into law
     (4)   anyone can formally propose a bill in Congress
     (5)   none of the above

1. 5 - All of these. The choices describe roles that political parties play in a democracy. While choice 1 may appear to be the most important reason, the question does not ask you to make such a distinction.

2. 3 - False, certain basic rights should be safeguarded. Although democracies operate on the principles of majority rule, they establish governments based upon laws. The inalienable rights defined by the Bill of Rights cannot be disregarded by the majority.

3. 3 - The right to a guaranteed annual income. The other choices are part of the Bill of Rights. There is no provision under the Constitution guaranteeing an annual income.

4. 4 - Veto a law. Following the arrow on the left going toward the legislative branch reveals that the President has this power. Congress may override a veto, the Supreme Court may declare laws unconstitutional and the people of a state or district elect members to Congress.

5. 1 - Checks and balances. Madison was writing in support of the U.S. Constitution. He warned of too much concentration of power and the need to counteract ambition.

6. 4 - A system of checks and balances. The reason for this answer is similar to the one stated above.

7. 5 - Gain greater control of school curriculum and policy. The regulation of schools falls under the responsiblity of each state government and their local districts. When the federal government gives money to schools it often relates to programs and policies. Property taxes are regulated by states and local governments.

8. 1 - Third parties have served no purpose in U.S. history. A key to this question is the underlined word "not". While the goals of the Liberty, Greenback and Populist parties at the time of their existence seemed radical, their goals were later realized. This can also be said of some of the other parties listed. The purpose of a third party in the U.S. is often to generate different ideas.

9. 3 - The Great Depression. President Roosevelt assumed office in 1933 at the height of the Great Depression. The speech excerpt describes conditions within the U.S.

10. 1 - Greater government involvement. His program which was called the New Deal increased the role of the federal government in fighting the effects of the depression and instituting programs to prevent future ones.

11. 5 - The fourteenth amendment protects citizens from violations that may be committed by state governments. Segregated schools have been declared as unconstitutional.

12. 1 - The searching of a person's home requires a search warrant that is provided by a judge who has been given probable cause by the police.

13. 4 - Certain groups may feel that the death penalty constitutes cruel and unusual punishment.

14. 1 - Approved by both houses of Congress. The U.S. has a bicameral legislature meaning that both houses must pass the same bill before it can become law. If the President refuses to sign a bill, but rather vetoes it the Congress may override it. At times, a committee of Congress will not approve a bill, but the majority of both houses will.

15. 2 - Much of the work is done by committees. There are thousands of bills introduced before Congress each year. It would be difficult for the 535 members (435 - House of Representatives, 100 Senators) to investigate each one. It is left to the various committees to research the merits of these bills. Only a member of Congress can introduce a bill.

ECONOMICS

Like the other social services, economics deals with the behavior and relationship of people. Economists try to collect as many facts as possible and to think about them logically. Their conclusions will not always universally apply due to the complex interaction of the activities, thoughts, emotions, habits and living patterns that they are studying.

In studying economics it is important to have an understanding of the scope of this social study/science. Below are three definitions of economics.

1. The study of how people try to satisfy their wants by getting the most out of their limited resources.

2. The study of man's wants and the satisfaction of those wants.

3. The study of how people produce and distribute the goods and services they want.

From these definitions one can see the scope of economics is broad. It includes consumption, production, exchange, distribution and public finance. Consumption is concerned with the manner in which goods and services are used up in the satisfaction of human wants. This could include eating food, enjoying the use of a television set, or receiving dental care. Production deals with the creation of goods and services like the manufacture of an automobile or the work done by a typist in an office. Exchange describes the conditions under which goods and services are bought and sold for money, credit, or other goods and services. Distribution involves how the money received from the sale of goods and services produced by a society is distributed among the various groups. Workers receive wages, landlords receive rent, a lender of money receives interest, owners of a business organization receive profits, and the government receives taxes. Finally, public finance describes how the government collects and spends money needed to carry out its various activities.

Economies can be generally classified into three categories: command, market, and traditional. Since a traditional economy is most closely associated with a primitive society, one finds in the world today economies falling under the broad heading of either a command or market economy.

Looking back at the definitions of economics reveals how societies must answer basic questions. They must determine:

    a.   what will be produced

    b.   how much will be produced

    c.   for whom it will be produced

In a command economy, these questions are answered by a person or group of persons representing the entire nation. Wages and prices are also determined by the government. The Soviet Union and Peoples Republic of China can be generally described as having command economies.

In a market economy, the answers to these questions are determined by buyers and sellers. What consumers will buy determines what will be produced. How much will be produced is affected by how much consumers will purchase.

In a traditional economy, people look to the past to answer basic economic questions. The items produced and the quantity is determined by what was previously done.

The American economic system can best be described as a "mixed economy". While many of its characteristics are that of a market economy there are features that include the government's involvement on the local, state and/or national levels. Those features that make the U.S. a market (capitalistic) economy include the right of Americans to own private property, start a business (free enterprise) and compete openly with other businesses to attract customers for the purpose of making a profit.

In reviewing the section on U.S. history you read how the government increased its role in the economy. Today the government owns part of the nation's resources. It operates some large businesses like atomic energy plants and local transportation systems. Regulations governing minimum wages, maximum hours and child labor are in force. In addition, prohibiting monopolies or providing false information fall under the government's scrutiny. Government agencies also inspect food, approve drugs, grade meats and establish safety standards for different forms of transportation. Finally, the U.S. plays a large role through its fiscal policy (power to tax and spend) and monetary policy (control of the money and credit supply).

One of the major economic concerns is preventing inflation. Inflation may be defined as a situation when the value of money decreases. This can occur when the supply of money is more abundant than the quantity of goods demanded. It can be described as too much money chasing too few goods. Inflation can also happen when prices rise because of increased costs (wage-price spiral).

Inflation is worrisome because it effects the purchasing power of people. Purchasing power is a method of expressing the cost of living in terms of dollars and cents. Groups of people that usually lose some of their buying power during inflationary times are creditors, savers, businessmen, workers and people living on fixed incomes. Those people in debt may benefit from inflation because the value of the money they borrowed is greater than the value of money they will have to repay.

Let's try a few typical GED questions.

Items 1, 2 and 3 refer to the speakers comments below:

Speaker 1: You are wrong if you believe the government can influence the economy in a positive way. Those who know best are the businessmen who fuel the economy by hiring workers and providing needed goods.

Speaker 2: The state should own and operate the means of production, as well as decide what should be produced.

Speaker 3: While making a profit is an important feature of a free enterprise system, some controls are necessary. Otherwise we might have consumers paying very high prices for basic goods and services.

Speaker 4: It is in the marketplace where the price becomes established for goods and services. This is how it should remain.

1. **Which speaker would most favor a command economy:**

     (1)   Speaker 1
     (2)   Speaker 2
     (3)   Speaker 3
     (4)   Speaker 4
     (5)   None of the above

2. **Which two speakers agree the most?**

     (1)   Speakers 1 and 2
     (2)   Speakers 2 and 4
     (3)   Speakers 1 and 4
     (4)   Speakers 2 and 3
     (5)   Speakers 3 and 4

3. **Which speaker would be in favor of legislation to limit rates insurance companies could charge for automobile insurance?**

     (1)   Speaker 1
     (2)   Speaker 2
     (3)   Speaker 3
     (4)   Speaker 4
     (5)   All of the above

4. **Which of the following would be considered an economic good?**

     (1)   sunshine
     (2)   lawyer's fees
     (3)   lawnmower
     (4)   haircut
     (5)   dry cleaning

Item 5 refers to the chart below:

What $100 in 1967 would be worth in selected years:

1970	$82
1973	$77
1977	$75
1980	$70

5. **How much of a raise per week would a person need in 1977 to equal the purchasing power he had in 1967?**

    (1)   less than $25
    (2)   more than $25
    (3)   no raise would be necessary
    (4)   less than $18
    (5) $75

Item 6 refers to the chart below:

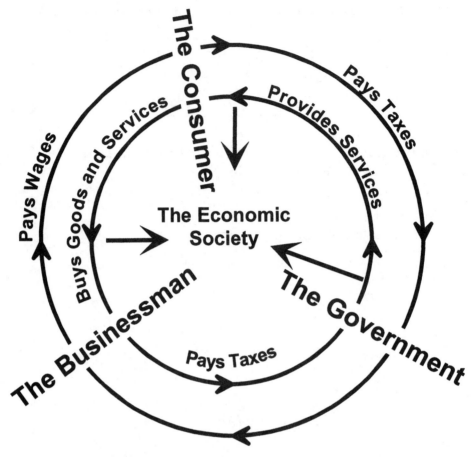

The Circular Flow

6. **The chart supports the view that:**

    (1) government plays a minor role in the economy
    (2) businesses benefit by paying taxes
    (3) only consumers pay taxes
    (4) government only provides services to consumers
    (5) all parts of the economic society depend upon one another

Items 7-9 refer to the graphs below:

Supply Chart for Candy Bars

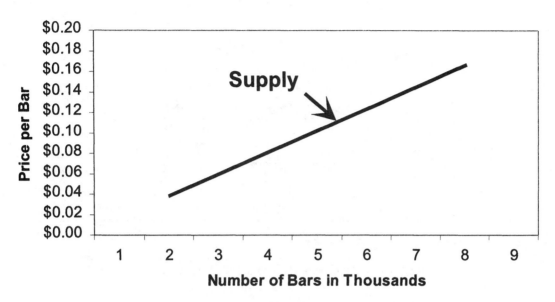

Demand Chart for Candy Bars

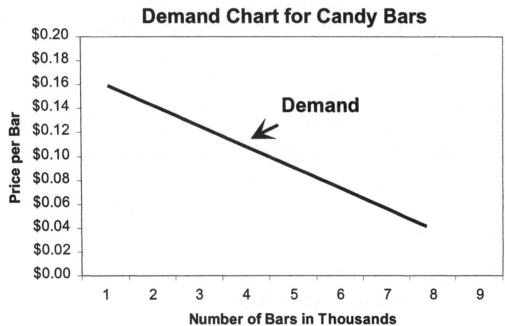

Price Chart for Candy Bars

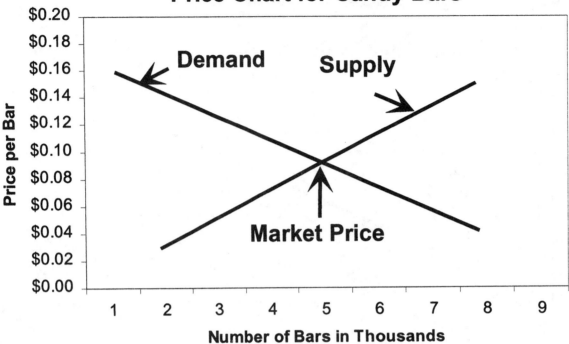

7. **How many candy bars will be offered at a price of $.04 per bar?**

   (1) 1,000
   (2) 2,000
   (3) 4,000
   (4) 8,000
   (5) 16,000

8. **How many candy bars will customers offer to buy at a price of $.16 per bar?**

   (1) 1,000
   (2) 4,000
   (3) 8,000
   (4) 9,000
   (5) 5,000

9. **The price at which supply and demand are equal is:**

   (1) more favorable to the producer
   (2) more favorable to the consumer
   (3) the market price
   (4) the supply price
   (5) the demand price

Items 10 and 11 refer to the pie graphs:

Where the Budget Dollar Goes

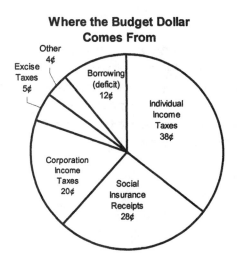

Where the Budget Dollar Comes From

Other 4¢
Excise Taxes 5¢
Borrowing (deficit) 12¢
Individual Income Taxes 38¢
Corporation Income Taxes 20¢
Social Insurance Receipts 28¢

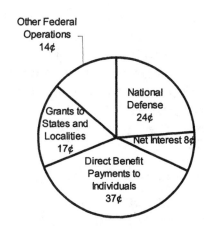

Other Federal Operations 14¢
Grants to States and Localities 17¢
National Defense 24¢
Net Interest 8¢
Direct Benefit Payments to Individuals 37¢

10. **The greatest source of revenue for the federal government in 1979 was**

    (1)   borrowing
    (2)   grants from states and local governments
    (3)   corporate income taxes
    (4)   excise taxes
    (5)   personal income taxes

11. **The federal government had a balanced budget in 1979. This statement is:**

    (1)   true
    (2)   the government had excess money in 1979
    (3)   false, defense spending was more than the tax on corporations
    (4)   false, the government had to borrow in order to meet its expenses
    (5)   cannot be determined from the information given

12. **Those who may benefit from inflation are:**

    (1)   people on a fixed income
    (2)   savers
    (3)   debtors
    (4)   creditors
    (5)   everyone

Items 13 and 14 refers to the passage:

In a free economy such as in the United States, the desire for profit is relied upon to encourage spending for production of goods and services. Such spending creates income for those who own the factors of production. Many economists believe, however, that the government can use certain policies that will stabilize and promote production and income. By controlling the supply of money and credit, as well as using its power to tax and spend, the government has the potential to play a vital role. However, it is important to note that to be effective, monetary and fiscal policies must be of the right type. They must be coordinated and they must be used at the right time.

13. The passage states that in the U.S. economy:

   (1)   profit is not necessary
   (2)   government should spend more and tax less
   (3)   profit is an important motive
   (4)   interest rates are too high
   (5)   is not affected by government policies

14. One could infer from the passage - if the government raised taxes during a depression the result would:

   (1)   always be correct
   (2)   increase consumer spending
   (3)   have no effect
   (4)   decrease consumer spending
   (5)   protect the economy from foreign investors

15. Economists focus their attention on the:

   (1)   process by which people make and spend their incomes
   (2)   effects of climate on clothing choices
   (3)   anticipated improvements in transportation and communication
   (4)   impact of school integration
   (5)   the role of two parent families

ANSWERS AND EXPLANATIONS - ECONOMICS

1. 2 - Speaker 2. This speaker shares the views of someone who would support the economic system found in the Soviet Union where the economy is run by the government.

2. 3 - Speakers 1 and 4. Both of these speakers favor a capitalistic (market) economy.

3. 3 - Speaker 3. This speaker looks to the government for regulation, but not total control.

4. 3 - lawnmower. A lawnmower represents a want that some people would be willing to pay. Choices 2 and 4 represent a service not a good while Choice 1 is in such abundant supply and does not require payment to receive.

5. 2 - more than $25. In 1977 the purchasing power was $75 compared to what could be bought in 1967.

6. 5 - all parts of the economic society depend upon one another. The chart reveals the interrelationship of business, government and the consumer. Note how the arrows flow in a circular pattern between the three groups.

7. 2 - 2,000. Use the supply chart to locate the answer. The lower the price the fewer items offered by the supplier (producer).

8. 1 - 1,000. Use the demand chart to locate the answer. Look for the $16 price and trace with your finger downward to line indicating the number demanded. The higher the price the less desired.

9. 3 - market price. Look at the third graph. This compares demand and supply as it relates to price.

10. 5 - income taxes. Look at the graph dealing with where the government receives its money. Note the largest single portion comes from individual income taxes.

11. 4 - false, the government had to borrow in order to meet its expenses. Note that the graph dealing with where the money comes from reveals that $.12 of every dollar spent was borrowed. It is also interesting to note in the other graph that $.8 of every dollar was spent on interest from borrowing that took place in previous years.

12. 3 - debtors. Since the value of money is less during inflationary times, the value was greater when it was borrowed compared to when the money was paid back.

13. 3 - profit is an important motive. The first two lines indicate the role profit plays in a market economy.

14. 4 - decrease consumer spending. If the government raised taxes it would take money away from consumers giving them less money to spend. This would not usually be correct during an economic downturn.

15. 1 - process by which people make and spend their money. This concerns economic matters while the other choices deal with geography and sociology.

VARIETY OF TOPICS AND ISSUES SOCIAL SCIENTISTS STUDY

This final section will present a variety of topics, issues, and trends that are important to consider in your social studies review.

POPULATION EXPLOSION

One of the most important issues facing the modern world is population growth. Consider that the estimated population of the world in 8,000 B.C. was about five million. The population did not reach 500 million until 1650 A.D. The one billion figure was not reached until approximately 1850, a doubling time of 200 years. The next time the world's population doubled took place just eighty years later. By 1975, the population doubled again to reach four billion people. Many projections suggest it will take only fifty years for the population to double again to eight billion.

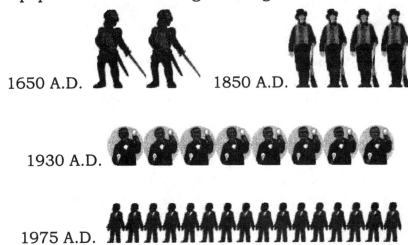

1650 A.D.   1850 A.D.

1930 A.D.

1975 A.D.

When examining population growth, nations of the world are divided into groups depending on their level of development, with respect to their industrial base, health care capabilities, literacy rate, and ability to feed their population. Those countries that have the most deficiencies in these areas tend to have the highest growth rates. Many of the nations in Latin America, Africa, and Asia fall into this developing group. More developed countries like the United States, Canada, Japan, Australia, and most European nations have relatively lower growth rates. In some cases the growth has actually stopped.

The time period that passes before a nation doubles its size also means the nation's resources must at least double to maintain the standard of living. In many countries like Bolivia and Ethiopia the standards are already inadequate. Hunger, malnutrition, and related diseases are the result of consuming less than the minimal daily requirement of calories. The majority of those that suffer are children.

Related to population growth is the areas people choose to live. Since the 1800's, many people in various countries have tended to migrate from rural to urban areas. However, urbanization is increasing at an alarming rate in developing nations. Such growth in these countries places great strains on the government to provide even the most basic sanitary services.

ECONOMIC INTERPENDENCE

One trend that marked the close of the last century is the growth in economic interdependence around the world. You may be familiar with OPEC (Oil Producing Exporting Countries), which is dominated by the oil-rich Middle East. These nations have banded together to control the oil supply and its price for the rest of the world.

Another example of economic interdependence is the European Union (EU). Already fifteen nations make up this body and they account for nearly 20% of the world's trade. Their goal is to promote economic progress and develop more freedom and security for its member nations, while also respecting the individual history and culture of each member nation. In 1999, the EU developed their own currency called the "Euro." Presently, they seek to expand their union to include nations in central and eastern Europe.

In the Western Hemisphere, the North American Free Trade Agreement (NAFTA) that took effect in 1994 between the United States, Mexico, and Canada created the world's largest free trade area. Its primary objective was to stimulate economic growth and give NAFTA countries equal access to each other's markets.

Finally, the rise of multinational corporations is yet another example of economic interdependence. These companies are permanently a part of what is already a global economy. Such companies act in terms of their world market share and not necessarily in terms of a particular nation or nations.

The interdependence between countries of the world has many implications. On a practical level, the problems in one part of the world often become the problems of another part. A term coined many decades ago saying that the earth is really a "global village" seems more true today than ever before.

POST COLD WAR

With the collapse of the Soviet Union in 1991, the Cold War struggle between the United States and the Soviet Union began to become a thing of the past. The United States emerged as the sole military and economic superpower. However, this does not mean there is world peace. Many issues remain that effect the world's stability. There is still a question as to whether or not the nations in eastern Europe (which were under former Soviet control) can continue toward a more democratic system and rely on a capitalistic market economy. In the Middle East, tensions mounted between Israel and her neighbors primarily over the question of a permanent Palestinian homeland. The rise of East and Southeast Asian economies, including the growing power of Communist China, raised important questions. In addition, the growing influence of arms merchants from around the world continues to contribute to instability not only in the Middle East, but also Africa and Latin America. Finally, the role of the United Nations in promoting world stability is an area that holds promise in the Post Cold War period. By the end of the 1990's, there were more than fifteen U.N. peacekeeping operations around the world.

UNDERSTANDING OTHERS

Every culture develops certain patterns taking the form of attitudes and customs. These patterns become familiar or natural to the people of that society. This helps the members feel a sense of unity toward one another. However, when a person judges other cultures by his or her culture's standards, it is called being ethnocentric. Such an attitude usually results in the person considering his or her own culture as superior (literally, at the center of the Earth).

Ethnocentrism can play a role in bringing about group loyalty and a respect for the roles in the society. However, when carried to an extreme, ethnocentrism leads to narrow-mindedness and intolerance towards others. In addition, such an attitude hinders people in their understanding of the customs of other people, as well as keeping them from having a deeper understanding into their own way of life.

It should be noted that ethnocentrism is not limited to a particular group or period in history. The ancient Chinese referred to all non-Chinese as barbarians. The word "barbarism" comes from the Greek and originally meant "a foreign way of speaking". Some traditional Eskimo groups used to refer to themselves as the Innuit, meaning "the people". This suggested that those who were not Eskimos were something less than people. In the United States, many people criticize other cultures where arranged marriages are prevalent.

Social scientists, particularly anthropologists, favor an attitude of cultural relativity. This is a view holding that all customs of a society be evaluated in terms of that society, rather than one's own. Cultural relativity requires impartial observations in its goal of explaining another's customs. Without declaring other ways of life as bizarre or inferior, people can still feel strongly and prefer their own behaviors and attitudes. Adopting such a viewpoint leads to mutual respect for each others' differences and provides greater opportunity for cooperation rather than confrontation.

The need to understand and respect others is more than something to think about. Among the greatest obstacles to a real sense of world community are the ongoing problems of racism and human rights. In some ways these two problems are separate, but they go together in the sense that they both show the inability or unwillingness of some people to recognize the dignity of others.

1. **Which statement reflects an ethnocentric attitude?**

    (1) "I understand why Hindus don't believe in killing cows, but I'm still going to eat beef."
    (2) "I like living in the U.S."
    (3) "I would respect them if they dressed in a civilized manner."
    (4) "I believe we could learn something from the way they treat their elderly."
    (5) None of the above

Item 2 refers to the graph.

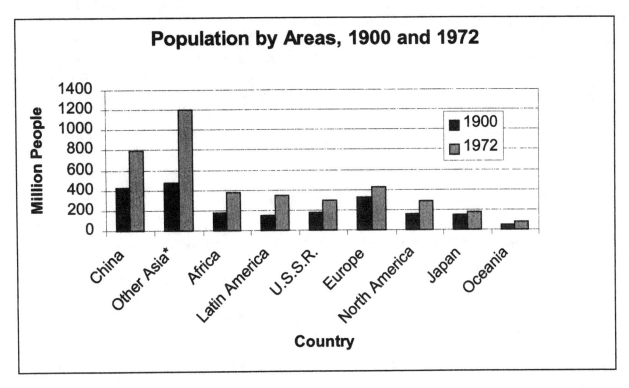

* Excluding Japan
Sources for 1900, by J. D. Durand. For 1972, SESA/BUCEN/ISPC, based on UN data (AID).

2. **The fastest growing area between 1900 and 1972 was:**

    (1) USSR
    (2) other Asia
    (3) North America
    (4) China
    (5) Africa

Item 3 refers to the graphs below:

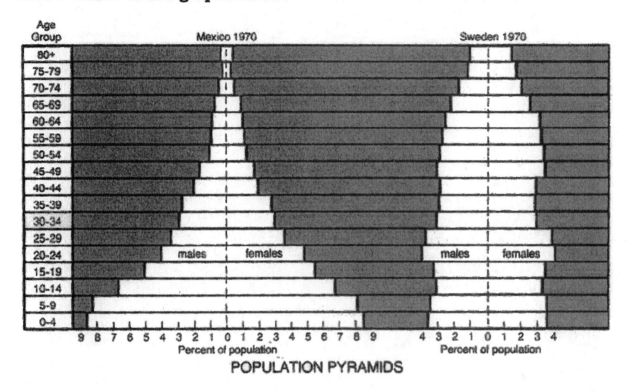

POPULATION PYRAMIDS

3. **Which statement is not supported by the graph?**

    (1)   life expectancy is longer in Sweden than in Mexico
    (2)   the population in Mexico is likely to grow at a faster rate than in Sweden
    (3)   the population in Sweden is more evenly distributed than in Mexico
    (4)   more people live in Mexico than in Sweden
    (5)   Sweden has a higher percentage of 5-9 year olds

4. **Which of the following is an example demonstrating economic interdependence?**

    (1)   U.S. automobile plant waiting for needed parts from a Canadian plant which is on strike.
    (2)   A drought in Brazil causes wheat prices to rise around the world.
    (3)   The seizing of the Saudi Arabian oil fields by another country.
    (4)   A domestic major textile manufacturer opening up new plants in two countries.
    (5)   All of the above

5. **The end of the Cold War seemed to offer renewed hope for world peace. The arms race between the superpowers came to an end, and western powers began to cooperate in offering help to the areas that once formed the Soviet Union and the nations it controlled Eastern Europe.**

From the above passage, a valid conclusion would be:

    (1)   The Cold War between the United States and the Soviet Union was an obstacle to world peace.

    (2)   The continued existence of the United Nations was no longer necessary.

    (3)   The rise of new superpowers in Western Europe would bring about a new arms race.

    (4)   The Cold War was really not over.

    (5)   None of the above.

ANSWERS AND EXPLANATIONS – VARIETY OF TOPICS

1. 3 - "I would respect them if they dressed in a civilized manner." This viewpoint suggests that ones person's way is acceptable while another way is inferior. The other choices (1 and 4) suggest understanding and choice 2 indicates preference.

2. 2 - other Asia. Looking at graph shows that this area almost tripled.

3. 4 - more people live in Mexico than Sweden. A population pyramid does not provide information on population size, but rather the distribution of a country's population based on gender and age.

4. 5 - All of the choices demonstrate or at least suggest that an event in one country as an affect on another country or countries. Each is an example show how countries are interdependent.

5. 1 - The author makes clear that the fact the Cold War has ended holds out the possibility for world peace. Choices 2 and 3 are situations not discussed at all in the passage while choice 4 is a direct contradiction of the opening line in the passage. To choose "none of the above" you must confidently eliminate the other choices.

IMPROVING INTERPRETATION SKILLS

While all of the GED Social Studies questions will be of the multiple-choice variety, many of them will call upon you to interpret visuals in order to select the correct answer. Visuals as graphs, photographs, charts, political cartoons, and posters are designed to convey information, usually without a great deal of text. Visuals represent another way to demonstrate your ability to analyze information, explore relationships, and determine the accuracy of data, recognize the meaning and/or apply knowledge in a different setting. Listed below are some strategies to help you correctly answer these types of questions.

POLITICAL CARTOONS

- You need to look beyond the literal in examining a political cartoon to find any symbolism that is being used by the cartoonist.

- If there are any words, read them carefully because they provide insight into the point of view being expressed and may clarify the symbols that are drawn.

- Take special note if the cartoon has a title.

- A political cartoon expresses a point of view usually dealing with some kind of a controversy.

Look at the cartoon on the next page. The author is pointing out how politicians tend to smile for the public, even when they are filled with fear and anxiety. In this case the politicians are (top left to right) Theodore Roosevelt, Woodrow Wilson, and William Howard Taft.

HOW THEY'RE ACTING—AND HOW THEY FEEL

26572

POSTERS

- Ask yourself who you believe is the intended audience for the poster.

- After identifying the audience, try to determine what the poster's author wants the audience to do.

- Look for both the visual and verbal messages being used.

- Like political cartoons, posters often use symbols.

Look at the poster below. The poster was issued during World War II by the U.S. government. The passenger depicts Adolph Hitler, leader of Nazi Germany. Using such an image provides one with some strong persuasion to car pool and show how every driver can contribute in a meaningful way to support the nation's war effort.

PHOTOGRAPHS

- Divide the photograph into sections and see what details become visible to you.

- Determine the feeling(s) you have from studying the photograph.

- From the people, objects and/or activities in the photograph make a conclusion as to why the photographer took this particular picture.

Look at the picture entitled "Girl at Weaving Machine" that was taken in 1908. At that time, children were used to work heavy machinery alongside adults in often poorly maintained factories. Restrictions on the jobs children could do, hours which they could work, and the requirements on attending school were made into laws in response to conditions depicted in this photograph.

GIRL AT WEAVING MACHINE

TABLES/CHARTS

- Look closely at the general topic being covered.

- Notice the headings for each column.

- The particular question usually only asks you to examine a portion of the table/chart, so you should focus on those particular areas or numbers.

Look at the table below and pay careful attention to the table's heading to compare the different dollar amounts in each of the various years.

Year	Amount
1970	$82
1973	$77
1977	$75
1980	$70

- There are basically three types of graphs. **Line graphs** are used to show the relationship of two or more sets of information. **Bar graphs** use bars to plot information instead of a line. They can be either horizontally or vertically presented. Both types of graphs are labeled on the bottom and to the left. **Circle graphs** are the third type of graphs. They are sometimes called **pie graphs**. They are used to show how an entire item/topic is made. The pieces of the pie/circle must add up to 100%.

- Read the labels carefully.

- Look for relationships.

- Use only the portion of the particular graph that relates to the question being asked. Look at the three types of graphs. Note how much information can be expressed in such a neat and organized manner. Think of the types of questions that could be asked based on the various pieces of information presented in the graphs.

Price for Copper, Zinc, and Lead

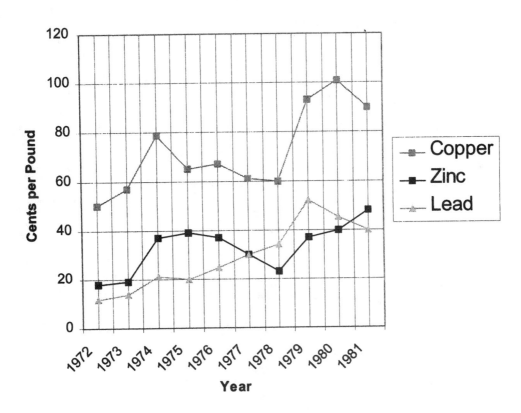

Coal Production

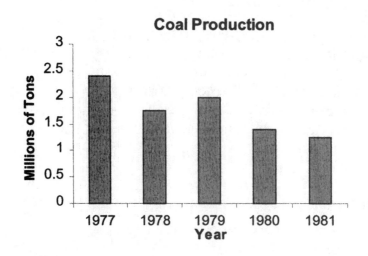

Who Gave to Charity

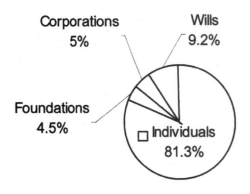

Who Recieved the Money

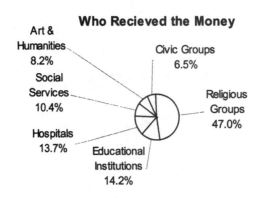

GED SOCIAL STUDIES TEST ANSWER SHEET

1. ① ② ③ ④ ⑤
2. ① ② ③ ④ ⑤
3. ① ② ③ ④ ⑤
4. ① ② ③ ④ ⑤
5. ① ② ③ ④ ⑤
6. ① ② ③ ④ ⑤
7. ① ② ③ ④ ⑤
8. ① ② ③ ④ ⑤
9. ① ② ③ ④ ⑤
10. ① ② ③ ④ ⑤

11. ① ② ③ ④ ⑤
12. ① ② ③ ④ ⑤
13. ① ② ③ ④ ⑤
14. ① ② ③ ④ ⑤
15. ① ② ③ ④ ⑤
16. ① ② ③ ④ ⑤
17. ① ② ③ ④ ⑤
18. ① ② ③ ④ ⑤
19. ① ② ③ ④ ⑤
20. ① ② ③ ④ ⑤

21. ① ② ③ ④ ⑤
22. ① ② ③ ④ ⑤
23. ① ② ③ ④ ⑤
24. ① ② ③ ④ ⑤
25. ① ② ③ ④ ⑤
26. ① ② ③ ④ ⑤
27. ① ② ③ ④ ⑤
28. ① ② ③ ④ ⑤
29. ① ② ③ ④ ⑤
30. ① ② ③ ④ ⑤

31. ① ② ③ ④ ⑤
32. ① ② ③ ④ ⑤
33. ① ② ③ ④ ⑤
34. ① ② ③ ④ ⑤
35. ① ② ③ ④ ⑤
36. ① ② ③ ④ ⑤
37. ① ② ③ ④ ⑤
38. ① ② ③ ④ ⑤
39. ① ② ③ ④ ⑤
40. ① ② ③ ④ ⑤

41. ① ② ③ ④ ⑤
42. ① ② ③ ④ ⑤
43. ① ② ③ ④ ⑤
44. ① ② ③ ④ ⑤
45. ① ② ③ ④ ⑤
46. ① ② ③ ④ ⑤
47. ① ② ③ ④ ⑤
48. ① ② ③ ④ ⑤
49. ① ② ③ ④ ⑤
50. ① ② ③ ④ ⑤

SOCIAL STUDIES SAMPLE TEST

DIRECTIONS*

The social studies test consists of multiple choice questions intended to measure general social studies concepts. The questions are based on short readings and often include a graph, chart, or figure. Study the given information and then answer the question(s) which follow. Refer to the information as often as necessary in answering the questions.

You will have eighty minutes to answer the fifty questions. Work carefully, but do not spend too much time on any one question. Be sure to answer every question. You will not be penalized for incorrect answers.

Do not mark in the test section. Record your answers to the questions on the separate answer sheet provided. Be sure all requested information is properly recorded on the answer sheet.

To record your answers, mark the lettered space on the answer sheet beside the number that corresponds to the question in the test.

FOR EXAMPLE:

1. **Early colonists of North America looked for settlement sites that had adequate water supplies and were accessible by ship. For this reason, many early towns were built near:**

    1) Mountains
    2) Prairies
    3) Rivers
    4) Glaciers
    5) Plateaus

The correct answer is "(3) rivers"; therefore, answer space (3) would be marked on the answer sheet.

Do not rest the point of your pencil on the answer sheet while you are considering your answer. Make no stray or unnecessary marks. If you change your answer, erase your first mark completely. Mark only one answer space for each question; multiple answers will be scored as incorrect. Do not fold or crease your answer sheet. Return all test materials to the test administrator.

*Directions used from the Official GED Practice Test with the permission of the American Council on Education.

DIRECTIONS: Choose the <u>one best answer</u> to each question.

1. **Country X established a government which provided for a representative democracy. Which of the following would one expect to find in this country?**

   1) one man rule
   2) a judicial oligarchy
   3) anarchy
   4) few rights for its citizens
   5) popularly elected officials

2. **Among the provisions of the Monroe Doctrine was the U.S. contention that foreign powers should not interfere in the internal affairs of countries in the Western Hemisphere. Which of the following hypothetical situations would most closely apply to this doctrine?**

   1) Japan invades China
   2) England and Canada sign a trade pact
   3) Poland attempts to exert political control over Nicaragua
   4) Germany violates the neutrality of Switzerland
   5) U.S. banks agree to extend credit to Brazil

3. **A protective tariff places a high tax on goods entering a country. Which group would be the most likely to oppose such a tariff?**

   1) domestic automobile manufacturers
   2) steel producers
   3) government officials seeking greater revenue
   4) consumers
   5) oil drillers

4. What is the main idea of this cartoon?

1) tariff legislation is empty
2) all the currency has been used up
3) anti-trust legislation spills through the cracks
4) anti-trust legislation is ground up by business interests
5) legislation can help businesses grow

Question 5 refers to the following quote:

"Only those Americans who are willing to die for their country are fit to live."   - Douglas MacArthur

5.   **The author of this quote would most strongly advocate**

1) an all volunteer armed forces
2) conscientious objectors
3) universal conscription (draft)
4) all of the above
5) none of the above

Questions 6 and 7 refer to the following information:

All societies regardless of size must respond to three basic economic questions. They must answer:

1.   how it will be produced
2.   how much will be produced
3.   for whom it will be produced

Listed below are three types of economic systems and brief explanations of how these questions are answered:

A.   **Market economy** - questions are answered within the marketplace between the buyers and sellers.
B.   **Command economy** - questions are answered by a person or group of persons who represent the entire population.
C.   **Traditional economy** - questions are answered according to what was done in the past.

6.   **In which type(s) could one expect to find consumers determining what will be produced?**

1) A
2) B
3) C
4) A and B
5) All of the above

7. In which type(s) could one expect to find wages and prices determined by the government?

    1) A
    2) B
    3) C
    4) A and B
    5) A and C

Question 8 refers to the following information:

In 1500, world population was approximately 425 million people. In 1999, the world's population reached six billion. According to the United Nation's estimates, the world's population will reach 8.04 billion by 2025 and 9.4 billion by 2050. More than half of the anticipated population growth will occur in South Asia and Africa.

Although population growth is still increasing, the overall growth rate has slowed. The annual rate of growth peaked at 2% in the 1960's and is currently at a 1.3% level. Continued slowing of the population growth rate depends on choices and actions during the next decade.

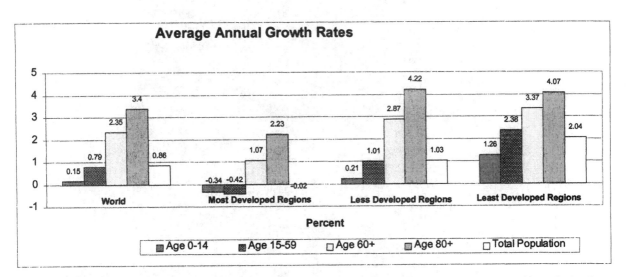

8. According to the information provided, which of the following is a valid conclusion?

    1) growth rates in the least developed regions are the fastest growing
    2) the world's population is projected to grow by 50% by 2050
    3) people are living longer worldwide
    4) the overall growth rate is actually declining in some countries
    5) all of the above

9. The last paragraph in Article I, Section 8, of the U.S. Constitution is sometimes referred to as the elastic clause. It reads: "To make all laws which shall be necessary and proper for carrying into execution the foregoing powers, and all the powers vested by this Constitution in the government of the United States, or in any department or officer thereof."

The statement below that best represents an application of the elastic clause is:

1) the president welcoming a foreign leader
2) Congress declaring war
3) The Supreme Court ruling on a legal matter
4) The president addressing a joint session of Congress
5) Congress passing a law that regulates the airline industry

10. The poster was meant to

1) show the horrors of war
2) encourage citizens not to complain about the hardships they might be facing because of the war
3) encourage more citizens to enlist in the armed forces
4) encourage citizens to join the peace movement
5) honor those that died during the war

11. The photo below was taken in 1931 showing people outside New York's closed World Exchange Bank. They were most likely

1) concerned about the status of their savings
2) wondering about the bank's hours
3) concerned with rising interest rates
4) worried about the war raging in Europe
5) wondering if their money was federally insured

12. **The oldest recorded legal system is the Code of Hammurabi which dates back to Babylon in 1700 B.C. The code contained almost 300 laws arranged under different headings. The basic principle behind the code was "an eye for an eye and a tooth for a tooth."**

   Law 142 dealt with a different subject. It stated: "If a woman so hated her husband that she refused to stay with him, her record shall be investigated at her city council, and if she was careful and was not at fault, even though her husband has been going out and criticizing her greatly, that woman, without incurring any blame at all, may take her dowry and go off to her father's house."

   From the above law, one can conclude that
      1) women had no rights under the code of law
      2) divorce was not permitted
      3) the society recognized at least some rights for women
      4) the code was only concerned with business and foreign affairs
      5) the code favored the rich over the poor

Questions 13 and 14 are to be answered by examining the viewpoints expressed below:

   Speaker 1: "I vehemently oppose any change to the existing order (status quo). These are the best of times

   Speaker 2: "While I favor preserving the status quo, there may be certain circumstances in which gradual change is necessary."

   Speaker 3: "I prefer to take a moderate view. A careful analysis should be done before taking an action on any proposal."

   Speaker 4: "Although my approach is not revolutionary, I am inclined toward change and reform."

   Speaker 5: "I advocate revolution as the only means to reach a peoples' desired goals."

13. **Which set of speakers hold the most extreme viewpoints on change?**

      1) Speakers 1 and 3
      2) Speakers 2 and 4
      3) Speakers 2 and 5
      4) Speakers 3 and 4
      5) Speakers 1 and 5

14. Which speaker would most likely support the violent overthrow of a government?

1) Speaker 1
2) Speaker 2
3) Speaker 3
4) Speaker 4
5) Speaker 5

Question 15 is based on the chart below:

UNITED STATES TRADE WITH THE MIDDLE EAST AND NORTH AFRICA
(SELECTED AREAS)

Country	Exports*		Imports	
	1976	**1977**	**1976**	**1977**
Algeria	487	527	2,344	3,228
Egypt	810	983	111	188
Iran	2,776	2,731	1,631	3,032
Iraq	382	211	123	420
Israel	1,409	1,446	437	590
Saudi Arabia	2,774	3,575	5,847	7,012

*Values in Millions of Dollars
Source :   Bureau of Statistics, International Monetary Fund
           Direction of Trade 1978.

15. Which statement is supported from the information provided in the chart?

1) Saudi Arabia was the leading trading partner of the U.S. in the Middle East
2) Oil is the leading trade product between the U.S. and these countries
3) The U.S. increased its exports to all of the countries listed between 1976 and 1977
4) Israel has a thriving trade with Egypt
5) In 1977, the U.S. exported more than she imported to the countries listed

16. Some of the jobs done by government bureaucrats are helping to collect taxes, running public services, processing forms and keeping records. A place to look for a bureaucrat would be

1) a U.S. government agency like the Food and Drug Administration
2) a communist government working in foreign service
3) a socialist government administering major industries
4) a military dictatorship reviewing applications
5) all of the above

Question 17 refers to the following statement:

> The absence of government will lead a society into chaos while a government that does not permit opposition will lead a society into tyranny.

17. A person who agreed with the statement above would likely favor

1) no government
2) a government where opposing views are discouraged
3) a government where different points of view are tolerated
4) a government based on one man rule
5) a government where there is only one political party

Questions 18 – 20 refer to the quote below:

DRED SCOTT DECISION, 1857

Now. . .the right or property in a slave is distinctly and expressly affirmed in the Constitution. The right to traffic in it, like an ordinary article of merchandise and property, was guaranteed to the citizens of the United States, in every State that might desire it, for twenty years. And the Government in express terms is pledged to protect it in all future time, if the slave escapes from his owner. . .and no word can be found in the Constitution which gives Congress a greater power over slave property. . .than property of any other description.

Upon these considerations, it is the opinion of the court that the act of Congress (the Missouri Compromise Act of 1820) which prohibited a citizen from holding and owning property of this kind in the territory of the United States north of the line therein mentioned is not warranted by the Constitution, and is therefore void; and that neither Dred Scott nor any of his family, were made free by being carried into this territory; even if they had been carried there by the owner, with the intention of becoming a permanent resident . . .

18. Which of the following is NOT a conclusion that can be made from the Dred Scott Decision?

1) a slave was considered property
2) the Missouri Compromise Act of 1820 was void
3) the issue of slavery was settled
4) the federal government has an obligation to protect the rights of slave owners
5) a slave, like the ordinary merchandise, can be transported

19. Which power was being exercised in the Supreme Court?

1) executing the law
2) declaring laws unconstitutional (judicial review)
3) sponsoring a bill
4) passing legislation
5) vetoing a law

20. Which of the following is the section of the U.S. that most likely would have favored the ruling in the Dred Scott decision?

1) the South
2) the West
3) the North
4) the East
5) all of the above

Question 21 refers to the quote below:

> "It became necessary for me to choose whether, using only the existing means, agencies, and processes which Congress. had provided, I should let the Government fall at once into ruin or whether, availing myself of the broader powers conferred by the Constitution in cases of insurrection, I would make an effort to save it, with all its blessings, for the present age and for posterity." – Abraham Lincoln

21. What is the author referring to in this passage?

(a) settling the issue of slavery
(b) saving the Union from states trying to leave
(c) abolishing the Articles of the Confederation
(d) making war against England
(e) rebuilding the government after war

Question 22 refers to the quote below:

"In every government there are three sorts of power: the legislative, the executive, and. . .the judiciary. . .. When the legislative and executive powers are united in the same person, or in the same body of magistrates, there can be no liberty. . . . Again, there is no liberty if the judiciary power be not separated from the legislative and executive. Were it joined with the legislative, the life and liberty of the subject would be exposed to arbitrary control, for the judge would then be legislator. Were it joined to the executive, the judge might behave with violence and oppression. There would be an end of everything were the same men or the same body. . .to exercise all three powers. . .."

22. What does the author of this passage support?

1) separation of powers
2) monarchy
3) multi-party system
4) a strong executive branch
5) dictatorship

Question 23 refers to the following passage:

Confucius, who lived during the sixth century B.C., is considered to be China's most influential philosopher. Although he never held a high political office, his teachings had great influence on Chinese civilization and political leaders long after his death.

One of his many sayings is the following : "Lead the people by laws and regulate them by penalties, and the people will try to keep out of jail, but will have no sense of shame. Lead the people by virtue and restrain them by rules of good taste, and the people will have a sense of shame, and moreover will become good."

23. From the above, it appears Confucius most wanted to:

1) improve society and government
2) establish a new religion
3) create more jails
4) abolish the need for political leaders
5) a leader should rule by fear

Population Growth of the Largest Colonial Cities

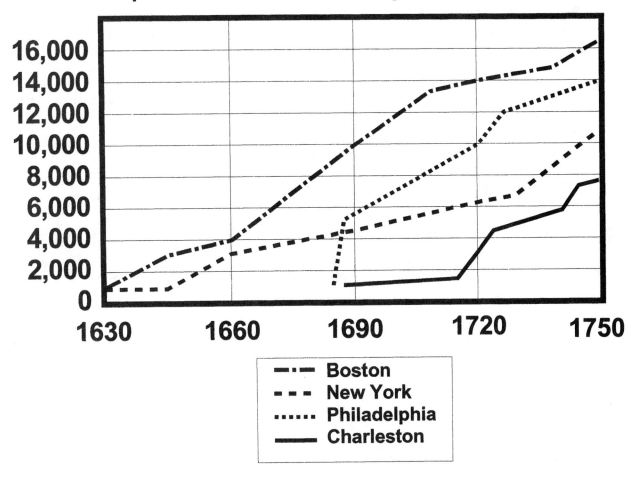

24. Which city led the population from 1630 to 1750?

1) Philadelphia
2) Charleston
3) New York
4) Boston
5) Data not included

25. Which city had not been founded by 1695?

1) Boston
2) Philadelphia
3) Charleston
4) New York
5) None of the above

26. In Western Europe, during much of the period known as the Middle Ages (800-1000 AD), a system known as feudalism dominated the political, economic, and social life of the vast majority of the people. Politically, there was a collection of strong local governments. The economic system was primarily based on self-sufficient agriculture while socially, a rigid class system existed.

From the above information, one can reasonably conclude that feudalism
1) still exists today in much of the world
2) encouraged the development of large-scale industry
3) provided people with some degree of protection and consistency
4) supported the democratic ideals of equal opportunity
5) all of the above

Question 27 refers to the graph below:

Women Employment Patterns : 1981

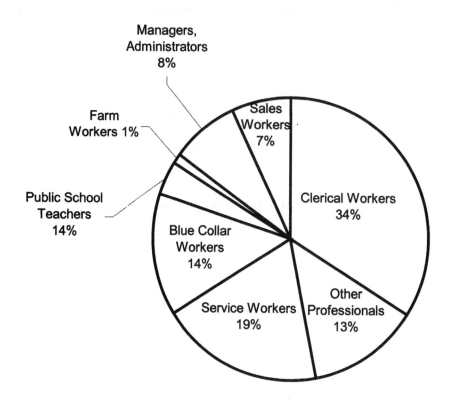

27. Which of the following statements is supported by the graph?

1) more than 25% of working women were either sales workers or service workers
2) more women were employed as public school teachers than blue-collar workers
3) the number of women entering service occupations has grown in the last five years
4) women prefer to work in sales than to be a manager
5) all of the above

28. "The real cause of the Civil War was slavery."

Which type of data would best support this statement?

1) figures which outlined the growth of cotton production in the South
2) figures on the increase in the slave population in the South just prior to the Civil War
3) figures on the growth of the abolition movement in the North and the anti-abolition movement in the South
4) figures on the increase in population in the North and South
5) figures on the number of states which permitted slaves

Questions 29 and 30 refer to the following (excerpted) speech made by John F. Kennedy:

What kind of peace do I mean? What kind of peace do we seek? Not a Pax Americana enforced on the world by American weapons of war. Not the peace of the grace or the security of the slave. I am talking about genuine peace, the kind of peace that makes life on earth worth living, the kind that enables men and nations to grow and to hope and to build a better life for their children – not merely peace for Americans but peace for all men and women, not merely peace in our time but peace for all time.

Some say that it is useless to speak of world peace or world disarmament and that it will be useless until the leaders of the Soviet Union adopt a more enlightened attitude. I hope they do. I believe we can help them to do it. But I also believe that we must re-examine our own attitude, as individuals and as a nation, for our attitude is as essential as theirs. And every graduate of this school, every thoughtful citizen who despairs of war and wishes to bring peace, should begin by looking inward – by examining his own attitude toward the possibilities of peace, toward the Soviet Union, toward freedom and peace here at home.

First: Let us examine our attitude toward peace itself. Too many of us think it is impossible. Too many think it unreal. But that is a dangerous defeatist belief. It leads to the conclusion that war is inevitable, that mankind is doomed, that we are gripped by forces we cannot control.

29. A good title for this speech may have been

1) "New Emphasis on American-Soviet Relations"
2) "U.S. is First: Now and Forever"
3) "Peace Through Strength"
4) "War is Inevitable"
5) "Pax Americana"

30. Kennedy believed that

1) world peace was attainable
2) people should seek out common traits between the U.S. and the Soviet Union
3) peace was important not only for the present, but for future generations
4) thinking that peace is impossible can lead to defeatist beliefs
5) all of the above

Question 31 refers to the graphs below:

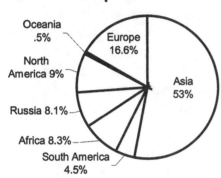

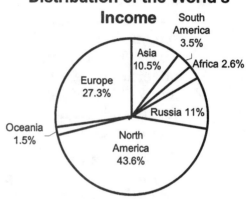

31. Which of the following can be concluded from these graphs

1) most people in the world enjoy a high standard of living
2) income is evenly distributed around the world
3) the typical Asian lives better than the typical North American
4) more than 60% of the world has less than 15% of the income.
5) None of the above

32. Distinguishing between fact and opinion is an important skill to learn. Which of the following statements offers a factual account of the origins of World War II in the Pacific?

1) On December 7, 1941, Japanese planes attacked the American naval base at Pearl Harbor as well as other American military bases. The next day Congress declared war on Japan.
2) The Japanese attacked Pearl Harbor because they were provoked by the U.S.
3) Had the U.S. not opposed Japanese expansion in Asia, Japan would not have attacked Pearl Harbor.
4) The U.S. needed a reason to enter the war so they used the attack on Pearl Harbor as an excuse.
5) Japan desired to prevent the U.S. from fighting Germany in Europe, so they declared war.

Questions 33 and 34 refer to the passage below:

In a market economy, advertising is a key tool in helping consumers purchase one company's product over that of another company. The reason why a consumer purchases a particular automobile, detergent, toothpaste, lipstick, or sweater often goes beyond the satisfaction of the item itself. Many people think about the status, beauty, and distinction associated with a particular brand.

While the main purpose of advertising is to create demand for a product, consumers pay for the cost of advertising when they by an advertised product. Expenditures for advertising in 1950 were almost six billion dollars and rose to over thirty billion dollars in 1978. The percentage of the retail price that goes to advertising varies. The average is a little over a cent for every dollar of sales, but can reach almost fifteen cents for brand name cereals and as much as thirty-five cents for certain cosmetics.

By stimulating demand, advertising makes possible the mass production of goods. Producers of nationally advertised merchandise can often afford to charge lower prices. Advertising informs consumers on the availability of goods and services in the marketplaces, as well as where they can be purchased.

Critics of advertising point out that sometimes advertising is misleading. Some also claim that it is often in poor taste. Beyond the fact that the cost of advertising is included in the cost of the goods and services is the feeling that the emotional appeal can lead consumers to buy products they do not need or cannot afford.

33. Which of the following would be an appropriate title for this passage?

1) "The Evils of Advertising"
2) "How Much Advertising Costs"
3) "Advertising: Information You Should Know"
4) "The Value of Brand Names"
5) "How to Purchase Cosmetics"

34. Which of the following is a conclusion that can be made from the passage?

1) consumers are not concerned with advertising claims
2) consumers make their purchases based solely on price
3) consumers pay the cost of advertising
4) consumers reject brand names in favor of generic brands
5) advertising is found primarily in those countries with a command economy.

Questions 35 and 36 refer to the following information:

Listed below are examples of federal agencies (created in part to offer consumers protection) and brief descriptions of their roles.

(1) **FOOD AND DRUG ADMINISTRATION** – protects consumers against unacceptable food, drugs, and cosmetics.

(2) **DEPARTMENT OF AGRICULTURE** – inspects and grades meats, fruits, and vegetables.

(3) **INTERSTATE COMMERCE COMMISSION** – approves rates for rail, bus, and water transportation.

(4) **FEDERAL AVIATION AGENCY** – establishes and enforces safety standards for airports and air transportation.

(5) **FEDERAL COMMUNICATION COMMISSION** – licenses radio and television stations.

(6) **FEDERAL TRADE COMMISSION** – acts against deceptive interstate advertising practices.

35. Consumers complaining about the rise in airline delays would most likely voice their objections to

1) Federal Aviation Agency
2) Federal Trade Commission
3) Interstate Commerce Commission
4) Department of Agriculture
5) Food and Drug Administration

36. Evidence of misleading automobile advertisements would most likely fall under the jurisdiction of

1) Interstate Commerce Commission
2) Federal Communications Commission
3) Federal Aviation Agency
4) Federal Trade Commission
5) Food and Drug Administration

Question 37 refers to the graphs below:

Contributions to Charities in 1982
Total: 60 Billion
Source: American Association of Fund-Raising Counsel

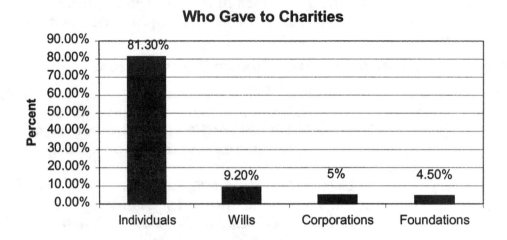

Who Gave to Charities

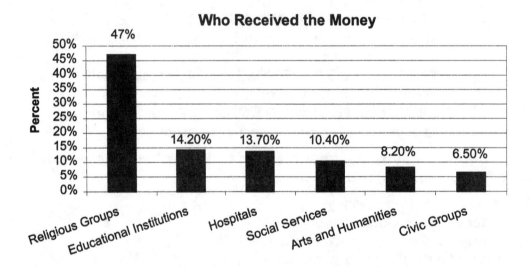

Who Received the Money

37. Which of the following is NOT supported in the graphs?

1) those who gave to charity were more likely to give to education than to social services

2) organizations that need donations to carry out their activities should depend on contributors from foundations

3) there are some people who plan on helping charitable organizations after their death

4) the amount of money donated to schools and religious organizations amounted to more than 60% of the total

5) all of the above are supported by the graphs

Questions 38 and 39 refer to the chart below:

Country	Area (Thousands of Square Miles)	Population (Millions of People)	Density of Population (People per Square Mile)	Income per Person in Dollars (Per Capita)
U.S.	3,615	203.2	56	3,910
Egypt	386	32.5	84	156
Iraq	173	9.5	55	255
Israel	8	3.0	375	1,470
Jordan	37	2.3	62	225
Kuwait	6	0.7	117	3,335
Lebanon	4	2.8	700	465
Saudi Arabia	870	7.8	8	310
Syria	72	6.1	84	215

38. **The Middle Eastern country whose per capita income is closest to the U.S. is**

    1) Israel
    2) Saudi Arabia
    3) Kuwait
    4) Jordan
    5) Egypt

39. **Which of the following is a conclusion that can be made from the charts?**

    1) most countries in the Middle East are more densely populated than in the U.S.
    2) there is a direct relationship between a nation's population and its overall size
    3) the smallest country listed has the greatest per capita income
    4) most people in the Middle East are involved in the oil industry
    5) most of the countries are allies of the United States

Questions 40 and 41 are based on the passage below:

The question of who should pay taxes is usually answered in two ways. The first is the **benefits received principle**, which holds that taxes should be paid by those persons who benefit from the way in which the money will be spent. The second is the **ability to pay principle**, which states that those who are able to pay, should.

40. Which of the following is a tax that reflects the ability to pay principle?

1) gasoline tax
2) graduated income tax
3) bridge tolls
4) Social Security withholdings
5) cigarette tax

41. The passage suggests that

1) taxes are too high
2) taxes should be paid by all Americans
3) taxes are based on two guiding principles
4) taxes are based on faulty principles
5) taxes are needed for governments to function

Questions 42-44 refer to the maps below:

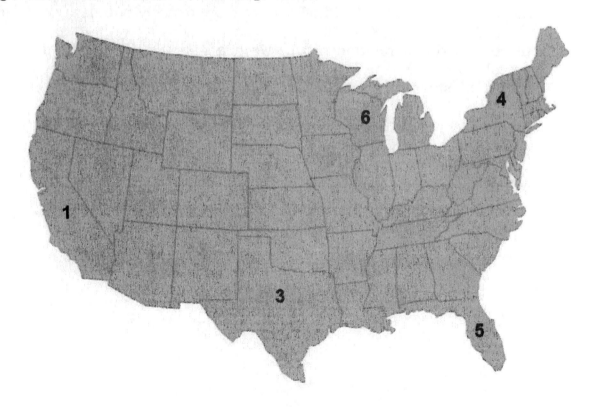

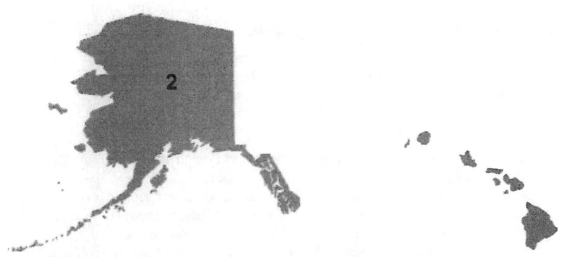

42. This state was one of the original thirteen colonies

    1) 2
    2) 4
    3) 5
    4) 3
    5) 1

43. This state is approximately sixty miles from Russia

    1) 2
    2) 4
    3) 5
    4) 6
    5) 3

44. This state has often been the first stop for Cubans entering the country

    1) 4
    2) 5
    3) 6
    4) 2
    5) 3

Questions 45 and 46 refer to the passage below:

During the twenties and thirties, radio achieved an important role in popular culture. Regularly scheduled programming began in the United States on November 2, 1920. Within two years there were over 500 stations and almost 1.5 million radios.

The magic of radio brought the world into people's living rooms. The radio offered live performances of opera and symphonies to people who had never heard classical music. Sporting events were vividly recreated by announcers for listeners at home. Radio also attracted large audiences who tuned in to their favorite weekly dramatic and variety programs.

45. The best title for this passage is

1) "Radio Brings the World to People's Homes"
2) "Radio Triumphs Over Television"
3) "World War I and its Effect on Radio"
4) "The Cost of Radio Programming"
5) "Radio in the Nineteenth Century"

46. The author suggests that radio is

1) caused by a breakdown in family life
2) lacked broad appeal
3) became an important source of entertainment
4) caused a decline in people's visits to the library
5) never became a force within America's culture

47. The U.S. has often been referred to as a model of cultural pluralism. In a pluralistic society many diverse regional, religious, and group cultures are tolerated. Which of the following is an example of cultural pluralism?

1) banning films produced in other nations
2) finding a variety of religious denominations within a single community
3) changing the name of sauerkraut to "Liberty Cabbage"
4) country clubs excluding certain groups from joining
5) segregating people by racial and ethnic background

Question 48 refers to the bar graph below:

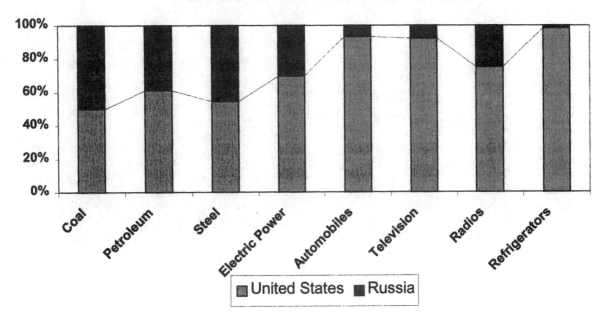

Russia and the United States A Comparison of Resources and Consumer Goods

48. Which of the following statements is NOT supported by the graph?

1) U.S. production of electricity is more than twice that of Russia
2) Russia is closest to the U.S. in the production of coal
3) Russia places more emphasis on the production of consumer goods than the U.S.
4) U.S. production of radios is greater than that of Russia
5) more Americans drive cars than people in Russia

Questions 49 and 50 refer to the map below:

GROSS NATIONAL PRODUCT 1964
□ Represents one billion U.S. dollars

49. **Which nation was the richest in the world as measured by the GNP?**

    1) United Kingdom
    2) United States
    3) Italy
    4) France
    5) India

50. **Which of the following Asian nations was the richest as measured by the GNP?**

    1) India
    2) Hong Kong
    3) Japan
    4) Philippines
    5) Republic of China

1. (5) Popularly elected officials. In such a country the citizens elect people to represent them in the government. Choices 1 and 2 suggests rule by either one or just a few people while choice 3 describes a condition where there is no government. Choice 4 is not a condition one would expect to find where the citizens are allowed to participate in the selection of their leaders.

2. (3) Poland attempts to exert political control over Nicaragua. Only choice 3 describes a situation where a foreign power (Poland) is interfering with a nation from the Western Hemisphere (Nicaragua). While choices 1 and 4 describe an interference, choice a deals with two Asian nations and choice 4 deals with two European nations. Choices 2 and 5 describe two nations agreeing with one another.

3. (4) Consumers. Such a tax would raise the prices of goods entering the country thus reducing the choices consumers have in making purchases. Choices 1, 2, and 5 represent groups who could benefit from less competition which higher prices would bring. Higher taxes would bring greater revenues to the government (Choice 3).

4. (5) The person in the cartoon is shown pouring different types of legislation into the pump. The pump is labeled business prosperity. This is called priming the pump. The amount of water (legislation) poured into the pump will be multiplied and come pouring out of the spout. The fact that two buckets (currency legislation and tariff legislation) are empty is not the main point of the cartoon. It is being implied that they have already been poured into the pump. Therefore choices 1 and 2 are not correct. If the legislation was being poured into a grinder and the legislation was negative to the business environment, then choice 4 would be correct. Since the exact opposite is true the correct answer is choice 5.

5. (3) Universal conscription. The quote suggests that those who want to live in America should be willing to fight for this country. Choices 1 and 2 give people an option on whether or not to serve.

6. (1) Market economy. The consumers are the buyers within an economy. In the two other types this decision is determined by either the government or what was produced in the past.

7. (2) Command economy. In this type of economy, the government officials control of these areas is related to their involvement in the other phases of economic activities.

8. (5) To correctly answer this question, you need to take advantage of the information provided in both the text and the bar graph. The text indicates the rise in projected population from six to over nine billion (an increase of 50%). A careful look at the bar graph reveals the other choices to be valid.

9. (5) Choices 1, 3, and 4 are not correct simply because they refer to the other two branches of our government, namely, the executive (president) and judicial (Supreme Court). It rests in Congress (Legislative branch) alone to make laws. The airline industry did not exist when the Constitution was written in 1787, but the "elastic clause" allows for Congress to make laws regulating interstate actions. Choice 4 is an original specified power given to Congress in the original document.

10. (2) To select the best answer, you need to not only look at the graphic scene being shown, but also carefully read the words printed on the poster. In this way you should note that the audience for the poster were civilians at home during the war. While they had to make sacrifices in doing without materials they might have had before the war, nothing they experienced would compare to the sacrifices made by those soldiers who gave their lives in combat.

11. (1) It is helpful if you note that 1931 was when the U.S. and most of the world had plunged into a severe economic depression. Bank closings were all too common and many who had money in those banks lost their entire savings. It was not until 1935 in the U.S. when deposits were insured by the federal government should a bank fail. You should also note the presence of the police officer standing guard outside the closed bank gazing at the three men looking in the window, suggesting his concern.

12. (3) The law clearly speaks to the fact that a woman had the right to sue for divorce and that it was not only possible to win, but also keep her dowry (the material goods given by her parents to the husband when she got married).

13. (5) Speakers 1 and 5. Although these speakers would agree on almost nothing, their viewpoints represent the most extreme positions on change. Speaker 1 is opposed to any change while Speaker 5 welcomes almost any change. The other three speakers fall between these two in terms of advocating change to the existing order.

14. (5) Speaker 5. This speaker favors revolution as a means to bring about change.

15. (1) Saudi Arabia was the leading.... The value of exports and imports was greater to the U.S. than the other nations listed. Choices 2 and 4 are areas not covered by the chart while choices 3 and 5 are not supported by the chart.

16. (5) All of the above. By examining the job done by a government bureaucrat, one can see that these jobs are necessary regardless of what form of government exists in a nation.

17. (3) A government where different points of view are tolerated. A middle position between chaos and tyranny is suggested by the passage. A government that allows for different viewpoints should prevent either extreme from happening. Choices 4 and 5 are similar to choice 2.

18. (3) The issue of slavery was settled. The Civil War started three years later. Rather than settling this issue, this decision intensified bitterness between the sections. The other choices are supported in the excerpt from this decision.

19. (2) Judicial review. By voiding the Missouri Act of 1820, the Court was exercising its power to declare laws unconstitutional. The other choices reflect powers given to the other branches.

20. (1) South. The vast majority of slaves lived in the South. This decision supported the right to own slaves.

21. (2) Saving the Union from states trying to leave. The word "it" refers to the Union. Slavery was secondary to saving the Union. Choice 5 is concerned with after the war. Lincoln had to first be concerned with preventing the fall of the government.

22. (1) Separation of powers. The passage describes the danger of having the various powers combined.

23. (1) The saying from Confucius tells leaders that if they follow his advice they will not only have an effective government, but also good (ethical) people. He suggests that this is the role of a leader as opposed to the other choices listed.

24. (4) Boston. Only Boston and New York existed in 1630. Furthermore, the line for Boston extends the highest to slightly more than 16,000 people by 1750.

25. (5) all of the above. Charleston was the last of the four cities founded, but that was prior to 1695.

26. (3) While aspects of feudalism may exist in parts of the world, it is by no means a dominating force. The idea of an economy based on agriculture where socially a condition exists where people are not likely to improve their status in society makes choices 2 and 4 poor ones. The fact that feudalism lasted for so long suggests that it met with at least some approval in satisfying people's basic needs with respect to food and protection. Remember once you are able to eliminate a choice as not possible it automatically eliminates an "all of the above" choice.

27. (1) more than 25% of the women.... Adding the two categories results in 26%. Choice 3 deals with information not covered in the graph while choice 4 makes a judgement not directly supported by the graph.

28. (3) Figures on the growth of the abolition.... Such figures would reveal the degree of hostility over the slavery issue between the North and South.

29. (1) "New Emphases on American-Soviet Relations". Kennedy argues the need to look for new ways to achieve peace. He emphasizes that this means developing a better understanding of the Soviet Union. The other choices suggest U.S. domination or a continuation of old policies.

30. (5) All of the above. Each choice is reflected in the passage.

31. (4) More than 60%.... The population of Asia and Africa was greater than 60%, but there distribution of income only amounted to 13.1%.

32. (1) December 7, 1941.... The other choices reflect opinions which can be disputed.

33. (3) "Advertising! Information You Should Know". The passage provides a variety of objective information about advertising.

34. (3) Consumers pay for the cost of advertising. The passage makes reference to the power of advertising, as well as the fact that it does cost consumers money. Choice 5 would be correct if it had said a market economy.

35. (1) Federal Aviation Agency. The FAA would be concerned with numerous delays because it might cause a safety hazard at the airport with flights arriving and departing.

36. (4) Federal Trade Commission. Deceptive advertising involving goods sold across state lines falls under the jurisdiction of the FTC.

37. (2) organizations that need to carry out.... Some foundations only contributed 4.5% of the total donated, it would be unwise for organizations to become overly dependent on them.

38. (3) Kuwait. The figure for Kuwait in column 4 is $3,335 compared to $3,910 for the United States.

39. (1) most countries in the Middle East.... Look at column three to verify this. The other choices are not supported while choices 4 and 5 are not covered in the chart.

40. (2) graduated income tax. This tax is determined by the amount a person earns. The other choices list taxes in which people derive some benefit (eg. roads, retirement).

41. (3) taxes are based on two guiding principles. The other choices contain opinions not addressed in the passage.

42. (2) 4. New York

43. (1) 2. Alaska

44. (2) 5. Florida

45. (1) "Radio Brings the World to People's Homes". The passage describes the new experiences people had because of radio.

46. (3) Became an important source of entertainment. The passage notes some of radio's contributions.

47. (2) Finding a variety.... Cultural pluralism suggests - be accepting of differences. The other choices are examples of rejecting differences.

48. (3) The Russia places more emphasis.... In all the consumer categories (autos, radios, etc.) the U.S. exceeds the Soviet Union.

49. (2) United States. Note the size in comparison to the rest of the world.

50. (3) Japan. Note the size in comparison to the nations in Asia. In both questions, you should focus only on the nations listed as choices.

APPENDIX A: LANDMARK SUPREME COURT CASES

In addition to the GED Social Studies Test possibly containing an excerpt from a fundamental historical document like the Declaration of Independence, U.S. Constitution, or one of the Federalist Papers, there may be an excerpt from a landmark Supreme Court case. Below are listed some important cases decided by the Supreme Court and a brief summary about the case.

Marbury vs. Madison (1803) – the decision established the right of judicial review, allowing the Court to determine whether or not a law is constitutional.

Fletcher vs. Peck (1810) – the decision marked the first time the Court declared a state law unconstitutional. All laws whether they are local, state, or federal must be in support with the ideas stated in the U.S. Constitution.

McCulloch vs. Maryland (1819) – the decision established the doctrine of implied powers, allowing for a rather broad view of the powers of the federal government.

Gibbons vs. Ogden (1824) – the decision allowed Congress the power to regulate (control) foreign and interstate commerce (trade).

Plessy vs. Ferguson (1896) – the decision allowed for "separate but equal" facilities, allowing for segregation to be legal.

Standard Oil Co. vs. United States (1911) – the decision forced the break-up of Standard Oil Co. of New Jersey under the ruling that it had unfairly used its economic power to severely limit trade.

Schenck vs. United States (1919) – the decision limited free speech in time of war, as the words expressed represent a clear and present danger to the nation.

Brown vs. Board of Education (1954) – the decision overturned the Plessy vs. Ferguson decision declaring separate but equal educational facilities to be unequaled, bringing about the beginning of an end to segregation.

Yates vs. United States (1957) – the decision stated that favoring an extreme philosophy would not be punishable unless it was proven that the accused was able to get others to take violent actions to overthrow the government.

Mapp vs. Ohio (1961) – the decision made clear that evidence could not be admitted in either a federal or state court by the prosecution if it was not obtained legally through a search warrant.

Engel vs. Vitale (1962) – the decision disallowed a prayer to be recited in the New York schools.

Gideon vs. Wainwright (1963) – the decision allowed for anyone accused of a crime to be represented by a lawyer, even if they could not afford one.

Miranda vs. Arizona (1966) – the decision required the police clearly inform the accused of their right to remain silent; anything they do or say may be used against them; they have the right to contact a lawyer and if they cannot afford a lawyer, one will be provided for them.

Roe vs. Wade (1973) – the decisions voided state laws that made abortions criminal offenses. It established that during the first three months of a pregnancy, abortion procedures must be left to the judgement of the woman and her physician.

Michigan vs. Sitz (1990) – the decision allowed the police to establish sobriety checkpoints.

IN CONGRESS, July 4, 1776.

The unanimous Declaration of the thirteen united States of America,

When in the Course of human events, it becomes necessary for one people to dissolve the political bands which have connected them with another, and to assume among the powers of the earth, the separate and equal station to which the Laws of Nature and of Nature's God entitle them, a decent respect to the opinions of mankind requires that they should declare the causes which impel them to the separation.

We hold these truths to be self-evident, that all men are created equal, that they are endowed by their Creator with certain unalienable Rights, that among these are Life, Liberty and the pursuit of Happiness.--That to secure these rights, Governments are instituted among Men, deriving their just powers from the consent of the governed, --That whenever any Form of Government becomes destructive of these ends, it is the Right of the People to alter or to abolish it, and to institute new Government, laying its foundation on such principles and organizing its powers in such form, as to them shall seem most likely to effect their Safety and Happiness. Prudence, indeed, will dictate that Governments long established should not be changed for light and transient causes; and accordingly all experience hath shewn, that mankind are more disposed to suffer, while evils are sufferable, than to right themselves by abolishing the forms to which they are accustomed. But when a long train of abuses and usurpations, pursuing invariably the same Object evinces a design to reduce them under absolute Despotism, it is their right, it is their duty, to throw off such Government, and to provide new Guards for their future security.--Such has been the patient sufferance of these Colonies; and such is now the necessity which constrains them to alter their former Systems of Government. The history of the present King of Great Britain is a history of repeated injuries and usurpations, all having in direct object the establishment of an absolute Tyranny over these States. To prove this, let Facts be submitted to a candid world.

He has refused his Assent to Laws, the most wholesome and necessary for the public good.

He has forbidden his Governors to pass Laws of immediate and pressing importance, unless suspended in their operation till his Assent should be obtained; and when so suspended, he has utterly neglected to attend to them.

He has refused to pass other Laws for the accommodation of large districts of people, unless those people would relinquish the right of Representation in the Legislature, a right inestimable to them and formidable to tyrants only.

He has called together legislative bodies at places unusual, uncomfortable, and distant from the depository of their public Records, for the sole purpose of fatiguing them into compliance with his measures.

He has dissolved Representative Houses repeatedly, for opposing with manly firmness his invasions on the rights of the people.

He has refused for a long time, after such dissolutions, to cause others to be elected; whereby the Legislative powers, incapable of Annihilation, have returned to the People at large for their exercise; the State remaining in the mean time exposed to all the dangers of invasion from without, and convulsions within.

He has endeavoured to prevent the population of these States; for that purpose obstructing the Laws for Naturalization of Foreigners; refusing to pass others to encourage their migrations hither, and raising the conditions of new Appropriations of Lands.

He has obstructed the Administration of Justice, by refusing his Assent to Laws for establishing Judiciary powers.

He has made Judges dependent on his Will alone, for the tenure of their offices, and the amount and payment of their salaries.

He has erected a multitude of New Offices, and sent hither swarms of Officers to harrass our people, and eat out their substance.

He has kept among us, in times of peace, Standing Armies without the Consent of our legislatures.

He has affected to render the Military independent of and superior to the Civil power.

He has combined with others to subject us to a jurisdiction foreign to our constitution, and unacknowledged by our laws; giving his Assent to their Acts of pretended Legislation:

For Quartering large bodies of armed troops among us:

For protecting them, by a mock Trial, from punishment for any Murders which they should commit on the Inhabitants of these States:

For cutting off our Trade with all parts of the world:

For imposing Taxes on us without our Consent:

For depriving us in many cases, of the benefits of Trial by Jury:

For transporting us beyond Seas to be tried for pretended offences

For abolishing the free System of English Laws in a neighbouring Province, establishing therein an Arbitrary government, and enlarging its Boundaries so as to render it at once an example and fit instrument for introducing the same absolute rule into these Colonies:

For taking away our Charters, abolishing our most valuable Laws, and altering fundamentally the Forms of our Governments:

For suspending our own Legislatures, and declaring themselves invested with power to legislate for us in all cases whatsoever.

He has abdicated Government here, by declaring us out of his Protection and waging War against us.

He has plundered our seas, ravaged our Coasts, burnt our towns, and destroyed the lives of our people.

He is at this time transporting large Armies of foreign Mercenaries to compleat the works of death, desolation and tyranny, already begun with circumstances of Cruelty & perfidy scarcely paralleled in the most barbarous ages, and totally unworthy the Head of a civilized nation.

He has constrained our fellow Citizens taken Captive on the high Seas to bear Arms against their Country, to become the executioners of their friends and Brethren, or to fall themselves by their Hands.

He has excited domestic insurrections amongst us, and has endeavoured to bring on the inhabitants of our frontiers, the merciless Indian Savages, whose known rule of warfare, is an undistinguished destruction of all ages, sexes and conditions.

In every stage of these Oppressions We have Petitioned for Redress in the most humble terms: Our repeated Petitions have been answered only by repeated injury. A Prince whose character is thus marked by every act which may define a Tyrant, is unfit to be the ruler of a free people.

Nor have We been wanting in attentions to our Brittish brethren. We have warned them from time to time of attempts by their legislature to extend an unwarrantable jurisdiction over us. We have reminded them of the circumstances of our emigration and settlement here. We have appealed to their native justice and magnanimity, and we have conjured them by the ties of our common kindred to disavow these usurpations, which, would inevitably interrupt our connections and correspondence. They too have been deaf to the voice of justice and of consanguinity. We must, therefore, acquiesce in the necessity, which denounces our Separation, and hold them, as we hold the rest of mankind, Enemies in War, in Peace Friends.

We, therefore, the Representatives of the united States of America, in General Congress, Assembled, appealing to the Supreme Judge of the world for the rectitude of our intentions, do, in the Name, and by Authority of the good People of these Colonies, solemnly publish and declare, That these United Colonies are, and of Right ought to be Free and Independent States; that they are Absolved from all Allegiance to the British Crown, and that all political connection between them and the State of Great Britain, is and ought to be totally dissolved; and that as Free and Independent States, they have full Power to levy War, conclude Peace, contract Alliances, establish Commerce, and to do all other Acts and Things which Independent States may of right do. And for the support of this Declaration, with a firm reliance on the protection of divine Providence, we mutually pledge to each other our Lives, our Fortunes and our sacred Honor.

APPENDIX B: THE UNITED STATES CONSTITUTION

We the People of the United States, in Order to form a more perfect Union, establish Justice, insure domestic Tranquility, provide for the common defense, promote the general Welfare, and secure the Blessings of Liberty to ourselves and our Posterity, do ordain and establish this Constitution for the United States of America.

Article I.

Section 1.

All legislative Powers herein granted shall be vested in a Congress of the United States, which shall consist of a Senate and House of Representatives.

Section 2.

The House of Representatives shall be composed of Members chosen every second Year by the People of the several States, and the Electors in each State shall have the Qualifications requisite for Electors of the most numerous Branch of the State Legislature.

No Person shall be a Representative who shall not have attained to the Age of twenty five Years, and been seven Years a Citizen of the United States, and who shall not, when elected, be an Inhabitant of that State in which he shall be chosen.

Representatives and direct Taxes shall be apportioned among the several States which may be included within this Union, according to their respective Numbers, which shall be determined by adding to the whole Number of free Persons, including those bound to Service for a Term of Years, and excluding Indians not taxed, three fifths of all other Persons. The actual Enumeration shall be made within three Years after the first Meeting of the Congress of the United States, and within every subsequent Term of ten Years, in such Manner as they shall by Law direct. The Number of Representatives shall not exceed one for every thirty Thousand, but each State shall have at Least one Representative; and until such enumeration shall be made, the State of New Hampshire shall be entitled to chuse three, Massachusetts eight, Rhode-Island and Providence Plantations one, Connecticut five, New-York six, New Jersey four, Pennsylvania eight, Delaware one, Maryland six, Virginia ten, North Carolina five, South Carolina five, and Georgia three.

When vacancies happen in the Representation from any State, the Executive Authority thereof shall issue Writs of Election to fill such Vacancies.

The House of Representatives shall chuse their Speaker and other Officers; and shall have the sole Power of Impeachment.

Section 3.

The Senate of the United States shall be composed of two Senators from each State, chosen by the Legislature thereof for six Years; and each Senator shall have one Vote.

Immediately after they shall be assembled in Consequence of the first Election, they shall be divided as equally as may be into three Classes. The Seats of the Senators of the first Class shall be vacated at the Expiration of the second Year, of the second Class at the Expiration of the fourth Year, and of the third Class at the Expiration of the sixth Year, so that one third may be chosen every second Year; and if Vacancies happen by Resignation, or otherwise, during the Recess of the Legislature of any State, the Executive thereof may make temporary Appointments until the next Meeting of the Legislature, which shall then fill such Vacancies.

No Person shall be a Senator who shall not have attained to the Age of thirty Years, and been nine Years a Citizen of the United States, and who shall not, when elected, be an Inhabitant of that State for which he shall be chosen.

The Vice President of the United States shall be President of the Senate, but shall have no Vote, unless they be equally divided.

The Senate shall chuse their other Officers, and also a President pro tempore, in the Absence of the Vice President, or when he shall exercise the Office of President of the United States.

The Senate shall have the sole Power to try all Impeachments. When sitting for that Purpose, they shall be on Oath or Affirmation. When the President of the United States is tried, the Chief Justice shall preside: And no Person shall be convicted without the Concurrence of two thirds of the Members present.

Judgment in Cases of Impeachment shall not extend further than to removal from Office, and disqualification to hold and enjoy any Office of honor, Trust or Profit under the United States: but the Party convicted shall nevertheless be liable and subject to Indictment, Trial, Judgment and Punishment, according to Law.

Section 4.

The Times, Places and Manner of holding Elections for Senators and Representatives, shall be prescribed in each State by the Legislature thereof; but the Congress may at any time by Law make or alter such Regulations, except as to the Places of chusing Senators.

The Congress shall assemble at least once in every Year, and such Meeting shall be on the first Monday in December, unless they shall by Law appoint a different Day.

Section 5.

Each House shall be the Judge of the Elections, Returns and Qualifications of its own Members, and a Majority of each shall constitute a Quorum to do Business; but a smaller Number may adjourn from day to day, and may be authorized to compel the Attendance of absent Members, in such Manner, and under such Penalties as each House may provide.

Each House may determine the Rules of its Proceedings, punish its Members for disorderly Behaviour, and, with the Concurrence of two thirds, expel a Member.

Each House shall keep a Journal of its Proceedings, and from time to time publish the same, excepting such Parts as may in their Judgment require Secrecy; and the Yeas and Nays of the Members of either House on any question shall, at the Desire of one fifth of those Present, be entered on the Journal.

Neither House, during the Session of Congress, shall, without the Consent of the other, adjourn for more than three days, nor to any other Place than that in which the two Houses shall be sitting.

Section 6.

The Senators and Representatives shall receive a Compensation for their Services, to be ascertained by Law, and paid out of the Treasury of the United States. They shall in all Cases, except Treason, Felony and Breach of the Peace, be privileged from Arrest during their Attendance at the Session of their respective Houses, and in going to and returning from the same; and for any Speech or Debate in either House, they shall not be questioned in any other Place.

No Senator or Representative shall, during the Time for which he was elected, be appointed to any civil Office under the Authority of the United States, which shall have been created, or the Emoluments whereof shall have been encreased during such time; and no Person holding any Office under the United States, shall be a Member of either House during his Continuance in Office.

Section 7.

All Bills for raising Revenue shall originate in the House of Representatives; but the Senate may propose or concur with Amendments as on other Bills.

Every Bill which shall have passed the House of Representatives and the Senate, shall, before it become a Law, be presented to the President of the United States: If he approve he shall sign it, but if not he shall return it, with his Objections to that House in which it shall have originated, who shall enter the Objections at large on their Journal, and proceed to reconsider it. If after such Reconsideration two thirds of that House shall agree to pass the Bill, it shall be sent, together with the Objections, to the other House, by which it shall likewise be reconsidered, and if approved by two thirds of that House, it shall become a Law. But in all such Cases the Votes of both Houses shall be determined by yeas and Nays, and the Names of the Persons voting for and against the Bill shall be entered on the Journal of each House respectively. If any Bill shall not be returned by the President within ten Days (Sundays excepted) after it shall have been presented to him, the Same shall be a Law, in like Manner as if he had signed it, unless the Congress by their Adjournment prevent its Return, in which Case it shall not be a Law.

Every Order, Resolution, or Vote to which the Concurrence of the Senate and House of Representatives may be necessary (except on a question of Adjournment) shall be presented to the President of the United States; and before the Same shall take Effect, shall be approved by him, or being disapproved by him, shall be repassed by two thirds of the Senate and House of Representatives, according to the Rules and Limitations prescribed in the Case of a Bill.

Section 8.

The Congress shall have Power To lay and collect Taxes, Duties, Imposts and Excises, to pay the Debts and provide for the common Defence and general Welfare of the United States; but all Duties, Imposts and Excises shall be uniform throughout the United States;

To borrow Money on the credit of the United States;

To regulate Commerce with foreign Nations, and among the several States, and with the Indian Tribes;

To establish an uniform Rule of Naturalization, and uniform Laws on the subject of Bankruptcies throughout the United States;

To coin Money, regulate the Value thereof, and of foreign Coin, and fix the Standard of Weights and Measures;

To provide for the Punishment of counterfeiting the Securities and current Coin of the United States;

To establish Post Offices and post Roads;

To promote the Progress of Science and useful Arts, by securing for limited Times to Authors and Inventors the exclusive Right to their respective Writings and Discoveries;

To constitute Tribunals inferior to the supreme Court;

To define and punish Piracies and Felonies committed on the high Seas, and Offences against the Law of Nations;

To declare War, grant Letters of Marque and Reprisal, and make Rules concerning Captures on Land and Water;

To raise and support Armies, but no Appropriation of Money to that Use shall be for a longer Term than two Years;

To provide and maintain a Navy;

To make Rules for the Government and Regulation of the land and naval Forces;

To provide for calling forth the Militia to execute the Laws of the Union, suppress Insurrections and repel Invasions;

To provide for organizing, arming, and disciplining, the Militia, and for governing such Part of them as may be employed in the Service of the United States, reserving to the States respectively, the Appointment of the Officers, and the Authority of training the Militia according to the discipline prescribed by Congress;

To exercise exclusive Legislation in all Cases whatsoever, over such District (not exceeding ten Miles square) as may, by Cession of particular States, and the Acceptance of Congress, become the Seat of the Government of the United States, and to exercise like Authority over all Places purchased by the Consent of the Legislature of the State in which the Same shall be, for the Erection of Forts, Magazines, Arsenals, dock-Yards, and other needful Buildings;--And

To make all Laws which shall be necessary and proper for carrying into Execution the foregoing Powers, and all other Powers vested by this Constitution in the Government of the United States, or in any Department or Officer thereof.

Section 9.

The Migration or Importation of such Persons as any of the States now existing shall think proper to admit, shall not be prohibited by the Congress prior to the Year one thousand eight hundred and eight, but a Tax or duty may be imposed on such Importation, not exceeding ten dollars for each Person.

The Privilege of the Writ of Habeas Corpus shall not be suspended, unless when in Cases of Rebellion or Invasion the public Safety may require it.

No Bill of Attainder or ex post facto Law shall be passed.

No Capitation, or other direct, Tax shall be laid, unless in Proportion to the Census or enumeration herein before directed to be taken.

No Tax or Duty shall be laid on Articles exported from any State.

No Preference shall be given by any Regulation of Commerce or Revenue to the Ports of one State over those of another; nor shall Vessels bound to, or from, one State, be obliged to enter, clear, or pay Duties in another.

No Money shall be drawn from the Treasury, but in Consequence of Appropriations made by Law; and a regular Statement and Account of the Receipts and Expenditures of all public Money shall be published from time to time.

No Title of Nobility shall be granted by the United States: And no Person holding any Office of Profit or Trust under them, shall, without the Consent of the Congress, accept of any present, Emolument, Office, or Title, of any kind whatever, from any King, Prince, or foreign State.

Section 10.

No State shall enter into any Treaty, Alliance, or Confederation; grant Letters of Marque and Reprisal; coin Money; emit Bills of Credit; make any Thing but gold and silver Coin a Tender in Payment of Debts; pass any Bill of Attainder, ex post facto Law, or Law impairing the Obligation of Contracts, or grant any Title of Nobility.

No State shall, without the Consent of the Congress, lay any Imposts or Duties on Imports or Exports, except what may be absolutely necessary for executing it's inspection Laws: and the net Produce of all Duties and Imposts, laid by any State on Imports or Exports, shall be for the Use of the Treasury of the United States; and all such Laws shall be subject to the Revision and Controul of the Congress.

No State shall, without the Consent of Congress, lay any Duty of Tonnage, keep Troops, or Ships of War in time of Peace, enter into any Agreement or Compact with another State, or with a foreign Power, or engage in War, unless actually invaded, or in such imminent Danger as will not admit of delay.

Article. II.

Section 1.

The executive Power shall be vested in a President of the United States of America. He shall hold his Office during the Term of four Years, and, together with the Vice President, chosen for the same Term, be elected, as follows:

Each State shall appoint, in such Manner as the Legislature thereof may direct, a Number of Electors, equal to the whole Number of Senators and Representatives to which the State may be entitled in the Congress: but no Senator or Representative, or Person holding an Office of Trust or Profit under the United States, shall be appointed an Elector.

The Electors shall meet in their respective States, and vote by Ballot for two Persons, of whom one at least shall not be an Inhabitant of the same State with themselves. And they shall make a List of all the Persons voted for, and of the Number of Votes for each; which List they shall sign and certify, and transmit sealed to the Seat of the Government of the United States, directed to the President of the Senate. The President of the Senate shall, in the Presence of the Senate and House of Representatives, open all the Certificates, and the Votes shall then be counted. The Person having the greatest Number of Votes shall be the President, if such Number be a Majority of the whole Number of Electors appointed; and if there be more than one who have such Majority, and have an equal Number of Votes, then the House of Representatives shall immediately chuse by Ballot one of them for President; and if no Person have a Majority, then from the five highest on the List the said House shall in like Manner chuse the President. But in chusing the President, the Votes shall be taken by States, the Representation from each State having one Vote; A quorum for this purpose shall consist of a Member or Members from two thirds of the States, and a Majority of all the States shall be necessary to a Choice. In every Case, after the Choice of the President, the Person having the greatest Number of Votes of the Electors shall be the Vice President. But if there should remain two or more who have equal Votes, the Senate shall chuse from them by Ballot the Vice President.

The Congress may determine the Time of chusing the Electors, and the Day on which they shall give their Votes; which Day shall be the same throughout the United States.

No Person except a natural born Citizen, or a Citizen of the United States, at the time of the Adoption of this Constitution, shall be eligible to the Office of President; neither shall any Person be eligible to that Office who shall not have attained to the Age of thirty five Years, and been fourteen Years a Resident within the United States.

In Case of the Removal of the President from Office, or of his Death, Resignation, or Inability to discharge the Powers and Duties of the said Office, the Same shall devolve on the Vice President, and the Congress may by Law provide for the Case of Removal, Death, Resignation or Inability, both of the President and Vice President, declaring what Officer shall then act as President, and such Officer shall act accordingly, until the Disability be removed, or a President shall be elected.

The President shall, at stated Times, receive for his Services, a Compensation, which shall neither be increased nor diminished during the Period for which he shall have been elected, and he shall not receive within that Period any other Emolument from the United States, or any of them.

Before he enter on the Execution of his Office, he shall take the following Oath or Affirmation:--"I do solemnly swear (or affirm) that I will faithfully execute the Office of President of the United States, and will to the best of my Ability, preserve, protect and defend the Constitution of the United States."

Section 2.

The President shall be Commander in Chief of the Army and Navy of the United States, and of the Militia of the several States, when called into the actual Service of the United States; he may require the Opinion, in writing, of the principal Officer in each of the executive Departments, upon any Subject relating to the Duties of their respective Offices, and he shall have Power to grant Reprieves and Pardons for Offences against the United States, except in Cases of Impeachment.

He shall have Power, by and with the Advice and Consent of the Senate, to make Treaties, provided two thirds of the Senators present concur; and he shall nominate, and by and with the Advice and Consent of the Senate, shall appoint Ambassadors, other public Ministers and Consuls, Judges of the supreme Court, and all other Officers of the United States, whose Appointments are not herein otherwise provided for, and which shall be established by Law: but the Congress may by Law vest the Appointment of such inferior Officers, as they think proper, in the President alone, in the Courts of Law, or in the Heads of Departments.

The President shall have Power to fill up all Vacancies that may happen during the Recess of the Senate, by granting Commissions which shall expire at the End of their next Session.

Section 3.

He shall from time to time give to the Congress Information of the State of the Union, and recommend to their Consideration such Measures as he shall judge necessary and expedient; he may, on extraordinary Occasions, convene both Houses, or either of them, and in Case of Disagreement between them, with Respect to the Time of Adjournment, he may adjourn them to such Time as he shall think proper; he shall receive Ambassadors and other public Ministers; he shall take Care that the Laws be faithfully executed, and shall Commission all the Officers of the United States.

Section 4.

The President, Vice President and all civil Officers of the United States, shall be removed from Office on Impeachment for, and Conviction of, Treason, Bribery, or other high Crimes and Misdemeanors.

Article III.

Section 1.

The judicial Power of the United States shall be vested in one supreme Court, and in such inferior Courts as the Congress may from time to time ordain and establish. The Judges, both of the supreme and inferior Courts, shall hold their Offices during good Behaviour, and shall, at stated Times, receive for their Services a Compensation, which shall not be diminished during their Continuance in Office.

Section 2.

The judicial Power shall extend to all Cases, in Law and Equity, arising under this Constitution, the Laws of the United States, and Treaties made, or which shall be made, under their Authority;--to all Cases affecting Ambassadors, other public Ministers and Consuls;--to all Cases of admiralty and maritime Jurisdiction;--to Controversies to which the United States shall be a Party;--to Controversies between two or more States;-- between a State and Citizens of another State;-- between Citizens of different States;--between Citizens of the same State claiming Lands under Grants of different States, and between a State, or the Citizens thereof, and foreign States, Citizens or Subjects.

In all Cases affecting Ambassadors, other public Ministers and Consuls, and those in which a State shall be Party, the supreme Court shall have original Jurisdiction. In all the other Cases before mentioned, the supreme Court shall have appellate Jurisdiction, both as to Law and Fact, with such Exceptions, and under such Regulations as the Congress shall make.

The Trial of all Crimes, except in Cases of Impeachment, shall be by Jury; and such Trial shall be held in the State where the said Crimes shall have been committed; but when not committed within any State, the Trial shall be at such Place or Places as the Congress may by Law have directed.

Section. 3.

Treason against the United States, shall consist only in levying War against them, or in adhering to their Enemies, giving them Aid and Comfort. No Person shall be convicted of Treason unless on the Testimony of two Witnesses to the same overt Act, or on Confession in open Court.

The Congress shall have Power to declare the Punishment of Treason, but no Attainder of Treason shall work Corruption of Blood, or Forfeiture except during the Life of the Person attainted.

Article. IV.

Section 1.

Full Faith and Credit shall be given in each State to the public Acts, Records, and judicial Proceedings of every other State. And the Congress may by general Laws prescribe the Manner in which such Acts, Records and Proceedings shall be proved, and the Effect thereof.

Section 2.

The Citizens of each State shall be entitled to all Privileges and Immunities of Citizens in the several States.

A Person charged in any State with Treason, Felony, or other Crime, who shall flee from Justice, and be found in another State, shall on Demand of the executive Authority of the State from which he fled, be delivered up, to be removed to the State having Jurisdiction of the Crime.

No Person held to Service or Labour in one State, under the Laws thereof, escaping into another, shall, in Consequence of any Law or Regulation therein, be discharged from such Service or Labour, but shall be delivered up on Claim of the Party to whom such Service or Labour may be due.

Section 3.

New States may be admitted by the Congress into this Union; but no new State shall be formed or erected within the Jurisdiction of any other State; nor any State be formed by the Junction of two or more States, or Parts of States, without the Consent of the Legislatures of the States concerned as well as of the Congress.

The Congress shall have Power to dispose of and make all needful Rules and Regulations respecting the Territory or other Property belonging to the United States; and nothing in this Constitution shall be so construed as to Prejudice any Claims of the United States, or of any particular State.

Section 4.

The United States shall guarantee to every State in this Union a Republican Form of Government, and shall protect each of them against Invasion; and on Application of the Legislature, or of the Executive (when the Legislature cannot be convened), against domestic Violence.

Article V.

The Congress, whenever two thirds of both Houses shall deem it necessary, shall propose Amendments to this Constitution, or, on the Application of the Legislatures of two thirds of the several States, shall call a Convention for proposing Amendments, which, in either Case, shall be valid to all Intents and Purposes, as Part of this Constitution, when ratified by the Legislatures of three fourths of the several States, or by Conventions in three fourths thereof, as the one or the other Mode of Ratification may be proposed by the Congress; Provided that no Amendment which may be made prior to the Year One thousand eight hundred and eight shall in any Manner affect the first and fourth Clauses in the Ninth Section of the first Article; and that no State, without its Consent, shall be deprived of its equal Suffrage in the Senate.

Article VI.

All Debts contracted and Engagements entered into, before the Adoption of this Constitution, shall be as valid against the United States under this Constitution, as under the Confederation.

This Constitution, and the Laws of the United States which shall be made in Pursuance thereof; and all Treaties made, or which shall be made, under the Authority of the United States, shall be the supreme Law of the Land; and the Judges in every State shall be bound thereby, any Thing in the Constitution or Laws of any State to the Contrary notwithstanding.

The Senators and Representatives before mentioned, and the Members of the several State Legislatures, and all executive and judicial Officers, both of the United States and of the several States, shall be bound by Oath or Affirmation, to support this Constitution; but no religious Test shall ever be required as a Qualification to any Office or public Trust under the United States.

Article. VII.

The Ratification of the Conventions of nine States, shall be sufficient for the Establishment of this Constitution between the States so ratifying the Same.

THE FIRST 10 AMENDMENTS TO THE CONSTITUTION AS RATIFIED BY THE STATES

The following text is a transcription of the first 10 amendments to the Constitution. These amendments were ratified December 15, 1791, and form what is known as the "Bill of Rights."

Amendment I

Congress shall make no law respecting an establishment of religion, or prohibiting the free exercise thereof; or abridging the freedom of speech, or of the press; or the right of the people peaceably to assemble, and to petition the Government for a redress of grievances.

Amendment II

A well regulated Militia, being necessary to the security of a free State, the right of the people to keep and bear Arms, shall not be infringed.

Amendment III

No Soldier shall, in time of peace be quartered in any house, without the consent of the Owner, nor in time of war, but in a manner to be prescribed by law.

Amendment IV

The right of the people to be secure in their persons, houses, papers, and effects, against unreasonable searches and seizures, shall not be violated, and no Warrants shall issue, but upon probable cause, supported by Oath or affirmation, and particularly describing the place to be searched, and the persons or things to be seized.

Amendment V

No person shall be held to answer for a capital, or otherwise infamous crime, unless on a presentment or indictment of a Grand Jury, except in cases arising in the land or naval forces, or in the Militia, when in actual service in time of War or public danger; nor shall any person be subject for the same offence to be twice put in jeopardy of life or limb; nor shall be compelled in any criminal case to be a witness against himself, nor be deprived of life, liberty, or property, without due process of law; nor shall private property be taken for public use, without just compensation.

Amendment VI

In all criminal prosecutions, the accused shall enjoy the right to a speedy and public trial, by an impartial jury of the State and district wherein the crime shall have been committed, which district shall have been previously ascertained by law, and to be informed of the nature and cause of the accusation; to be confronted with the witnesses against him; to have compulsory process for obtaining witnesses in his favor, and to have the Assistance of Counsel for his defence.

Amendment VII

In suits at common law, where the value in controversy shall exceed twenty dollars, the right of trial by jury shall be preserved, and no fact tried by a jury, shall be otherwise reexamined in any Court of the United States, than according to the rules of the common law.

Amendment VIII

Excessive bail shall not be required, nor excessive fines imposed, nor cruel and unusual punishments inflicted.

Amendment IX

The enumeration in the Constitution, of certain rights, shall not be construed to deny or disparage others retained by the people.

Amendment X

The powers not delegated to the United States by the Constitution, nor prohibited by it to the States, are reserved to the States respectively, or to the people.

APPENDIX D:
THE REST OF THE CONSTITUTIONAL AMENDMENTS

AMENDMENT XI

Passed by Congress March 4, 1794. Ratified February 7, 1795.

(Article III, section 2, of the Constitution was modified by amendment 11.)

The Judicial power of the United States shall not be construed to extend to any suit in law or equity, commenced or prosecuted against one of the United States by Citizens of another State, or by Citizens or Subjects of any Foreign State.

AMENDMENT XII

Passed by Congress December 9, 1803. Ratified June 15, 1804.

(A portion of Article II, section 1 of the Constitution was superseded by the 12th amendment.)

The Electors shall meet in their respective states and vote by ballot for President and Vice-President, one of whom, at least, shall not be an inhabitant of the same state with themselves; they shall name in their ballots the person voted for as President, and in distinct ballots the person voted for as Vice-President, and they shall make distinct lists of all persons voted for as President, and of all persons voted for as Vice-President, and of the number of votes for each, which lists they shall sign and certify, and transmit sealed to the seat of the government of the United States, directed to the President of the Senate; -- the President of the Senate shall, in the presence of the Senate and House of Representatives, open all the certificates and the votes shall then be counted; -- The person having the greatest number of votes for President, shall be the President, if such number be a majority of the whole number of Electors appointed; and if no person have such majority, then from the persons having the highest numbers not exceeding three on the list of those voted for as President, the House of Representatives shall choose immediately, by ballot, the President. But in choosing the President, the votes shall be taken by states, the representation from each state having one vote; a quorum for this purpose shall consist of a member or members from two-thirds of the states, and a majority of all the states shall be necessary to a choice. [And if the House of Representatives shall not choose a President whenever the right of choice shall devolve upon them, before the fourth day of March next following, then the Vice-President shall act as President, as in case of the death or other constitutional disability of the President. --]* The person having the greatest number of votes as Vice-President, shall be the Vice-President, if such number be a majority of the whole number of Electors appointed, and if no person have a majority, then from the two highest numbers on the list, the Senate shall choose the Vice-President; a quorum for the purpose shall consist of two-thirds of the whole number of Senators, and a majority of the whole number shall be necessary to a choice. But no person constitutionally ineligible to the office of President shall be eligible to that of Vice-President of the United States.

*Superseded by section 3 of the 20th amendment.

AMENDMENT XIII

Passed by Congress January 31, 1865. Ratified December 6, 1865.

(A portion of Article IV, section 2, of the Constitution was superseded by the 13th amendment.)

Section 1.

Neither slavery nor involuntary servitude, except as a punishment for crime whereof the party shall have been duly convicted, shall exist within the United States, or any place subject to their jurisdiction.

Section 2.

Congress shall have power to enforce this article by appropriate legislation.

AMENDMENT XIV

Passed by Congress June 13, 1866. Ratified July 9, 1868.

(Article I, section 2, of the Constitution was modified by section 2 of the 14th amendment.)

Section 1.

All persons born or naturalized in the United States, and subject to the jurisdiction thereof, are citizens of the United States and of the State wherein they reside. No State shall make or enforce any law which shall abridge the privileges or immunities of citizens of the United States; nor shall any State deprive any person of life, liberty, or property, without due process of law; nor deny to any person within its jurisdiction the equal protection of the laws.

Section 2.

Representatives shall be apportioned among the several States according to their respective numbers, counting the whole number of persons in each State, excluding Indians not taxed. But when the right to vote at any election for the choice of electors for President and Vice-President of the United States, Representatives in Congress, the Executive and Judicial officers of a State, or the members of the Legislature thereof, is denied to any of the male inhabitants of such

State, being twenty-one years of age,* and citizens of the United States, or in any way abridged, except for participation in rebellion, or other crime, the basis of representation therein shall be reduced in the proportion which the number of such male citizens shall bear to the whole number of male citizens twenty-one years of age in such State.

Section 3.

No person shall be a Senator or Representative in Congress, or elector of President and Vice-President, or hold any office, civil or military, under the United States, or under any State, who, having previously taken an oath, as a member of Congress, or as an officer of the United States, or as a member of any State legislature, or as an executive or judicial officer of any State, to support the Constitution of the United States, shall have engaged in insurrection or rebellion against the same, or given aid or comfort to the enemies thereof. But Congress may by a vote of two-thirds of each House, remove such disability.

Section 4.

The validity of the public debt of the United States, authorized by law, including debts incurred for payment of pensions and bounties for services in suppressing insurrection or rebellion, shall not be questioned. But neither the United States nor any State shall assume or pay any debt or obligation incurred in aid of insurrection or rebellion against the United States, or any claim for the loss or emancipation of any slave; but all such debts, obligations and claims shall be held illegal and void.

Section 5.

The Congress shall have the power to enforce, by appropriate legislation, the provisions of this article.

*Changed by section 1 of the 26th amendment.

AMENDMENT XV

Passed by Congress February 26, 1869. Ratified February 3, 1870.

Section 1.

The right of citizens of the United States to vote shall not be denied or abridged by the United States or by any State on account of race, color, or previous condition of servitude--

Section 2.

The Congress shall have the power to enforce this article by appropriate legislation.

AMENDMENT XVI

Passed by Congress July 2, 1909. Ratified February 3, 1913.

(Article I, section 9, of the Constitution was modified by amendment 16.)

The Congress shall have power to lay and collect taxes on incomes, from whatever source derived, without apportionment among the several States, and without regard to any census or enumeration.

AMENDMENT XVII

Passed by Congress May 13, 1912. Ratified April 8, 1913.

(Article I, section 3, of the Constitution was modified by the 17th amendment.)

The Senate of the United States shall be composed of two Senators from each State, elected by the people thereof, for six years; and each Senator shall have one vote. The electors in each State shall have the qualifications requisite for electors of the most numerous branch of the State legislatures.

When vacancies happen in the representation of any State in the Senate, the executive authority of such State shall issue writs of election to fill such vacancies: *Provided*, That the legislature of any State may empower the executive thereof to make temporary appointments until the people fill the vacancies by election as the legislature may direct.

This amendment shall not be so construed as to affect the election or term of any Senator chosen before it becomes valid as part of the Constitution.

AMENDMENT XVIII

Passed by Congress December 18, 1917. Ratified January 16, 1919.
Repealed by amendment 21.

Section 1.

After one year from the ratification of this article the manufacture, sale, or transportation of intoxicating liquors within, the importation thereof into, or the exportation thereof from the United States and all territory subject to the jurisdiction thereof for beverage purposes is hereby prohibited.

Section 2.

The Congress and the several States shall have concurrent power to enforce this article by appropriate legislation.

Section 3.

This article shall be inoperative unless it shall have been ratified as an amendment to the Constitution by the legislatures of the several States, as provided in the Constitution, within seven years from the date of the submission hereof to the States by the Congress.

AMENDMENT XIX

Passed by Congress June 4, 1919. Ratified August 18, 1920.

The right of citizens of the United States to vote shall not be denied or abridged by the United States or by any State on account of sex.

Congress shall have power to enforce this article by appropriate legislation.

AMENDMENT XX

Passed by Congress March 2, 1932. Ratified January 23, 1933.

(Article I, section 4, of the Constitution was modified by section 2 of this amendment. In addition, a portion of the 12th amendment was superseded by section 3.)

Section 1.

The terms of the President and the Vice President shall end at noon on the 20th day of January, and the terms of Senators and Representatives at noon on the 3d day of January, of the years in which such terms would have ended if this article had not been ratified; and the terms of their successors shall then begin.

Section 2.

The Congress shall assemble at least once in every year, and such meeting shall begin at noon on the 3d day of January, unless they shall by law appoint a different day.

Section 3.

If, at the time fixed for the beginning of the term of the President, the President elect shall have died, the Vice President elect shall become President. If a President shall not have been chosen before the time fixed for the beginning of his term, or if the President elect shall have failed to qualify, then the Vice President elect shall act as President until a President shall have qualified; and the Congress may by law provide for the case wherein neither a President elect nor a Vice President shall have qualified, declaring who shall then act as President, or the manner in which one who is to act shall be selected, and such person shall act accordingly until a President or Vice President shall have qualified.

Section 4.

The Congress may by law provide for the case of the death of any of the persons from whom the House of Representatives may choose a President whenever the right of choice shall have devolved upon them, and for the case of the death of any of the persons from whom the Senate may choose a Vice President whenever the right of choice shall have devolved upon them.

Section 5.

Sections 1 and 2 shall take effect on the 15th day of October following the ratification of this article.

Section 6.

This article shall be inoperative unless it shall have been ratified as an amendment to the Constitution by the legislatures of three-fourths of the several States within seven years from the date of its submission.

AMENDMENT XXI

Passed by Congress February 20, 1933. Ratified December 5, 1933.

Section 1.

The eighteenth article of amendment to the Constitution of the United States is hereby repealed.

Section 2.

The transportation or importation into any State, Territory, or Possession of the United States for delivery or use therein of intoxicating liquors, in violation of the laws thereof, is hereby prohibited.

Section 3.

This article shall be inoperative unless it shall have been ratified as an amendment to the Constitution by conventions in the several States, as provided in the Constitution, within seven years from the date of the submission hereof to the States by the Congress.

AMENDMENT XXII

Passed by Congress March 21, 1947. Ratified February 27, 1951.

Section 1.

No person shall be elected to the office of the President more than twice, and no person who has held the office of President, or acted as President, for more than two years of a term to which some other person was elected President shall be elected to the office of President more than once. But this Article shall not apply to any person holding the office of President when this Article was proposed by Congress, and shall not prevent any person who may be holding the office of President, or acting as President, during the term within which this Article becomes operative from holding the office of President or acting as President during the remainder of such term.

Section 2.

This article shall be inoperative unless it shall have been ratified as an amendment to the Constitution by the legislatures of three-fourths of the several States within seven years from the date of its submission to the States by the Congress.

AMENDMENT XXIII

Passed by Congress June 16, 1960. Ratified March 29, 1961.

Section 1.

The District constituting the seat of Government of the United States shall appoint in such manner as Congress may direct:

A number of electors of President and Vice President equal to the whole number of Senators and Representatives in Congress to which the District would be entitled if it were a State, but in no event more than the least populous State; they shall be in addition to those appointed by the States, but they shall be considered, for the purposes of the election of President and Vice President, to be electors appointed by a State; and they shall meet in the District and perform such duties as provided by the twelfth article of amendment.

Section 2.

The Congress shall have power to enforce this article by appropriate legislation.

AMENDMENT XXIV

Passed by Congress August 27, 1962. Ratified January 23, 1964.

Section 1.

The right of citizens of the United States to vote in any primary or other election for President or Vice President, for electors for President or Vice President, or for Senator or Representative in Congress, shall not be denied or abridged by the United States or any State by reason of failure to pay poll tax or other tax.

Section 2.

The Congress shall have power to enforce this article by appropriate legislation.

AMENDMENT XXV

Passed by Congress July 6, 1965. Ratified February 10, 1967.

(Article II, section 1, of the Constitution was affected by the 25th amendment.)

Section 1.

In case of the removal of the President from office or of his death or resignation, the Vice President shall become President.

Section 2.

Whenever there is a vacancy in the office of the Vice President, the President shall nominate a Vice President who shall take office upon confirmation by a majority vote of both Houses of Congress.

Section 3.

Whenever the President transmits to the President pro tempore of the Senate and the Speaker of the House of Representatives his written declaration that he is unable to discharge the powers and duties of his office, and until he transmits to them a written declaration to the contrary, such powers and duties shall be discharged by the Vice President as Acting President.

Section 4.

Whenever the Vice President and a majority of either the principal officers of the executive departments or of such other body as Congress may by law provide, transmit to the President pro tempore of the Senate and the Speaker of the House of Representatives their written declaration that the President is unable to discharge the powers and duties of his office, the Vice President shall immediately assume the powers and duties of the office as Acting President.

Thereafter, when the President transmits to the President pro tempore of the Senate and the Speaker of the House of Representatives his written declaration that no inability exists, he shall resume the powers and duties of his office unless the Vice President and a majority of either the principal officers of the executive department or of such other body as Congress may by law provide, transmit within four days to the President pro tempore of the Senate and the Speaker of the House of Representatives their written declaration that the President is unable to discharge the powers and duties of his office. Thereupon Congress shall decide the issue, assembling within forty-eight hours for that purpose if not in session. If the Congress, within twenty-one days after receipt of the latter written declaration, or, if Congress is not in session, within twenty-one days after Congress is required to assemble, determines by two-thirds vote of both Houses that the President is unable to discharge the powers and duties of his office, the Vice President shall continue to discharge the same as Acting President; otherwise, the President shall resume the powers and duties of his office.

AMENDMENT XXVI

Passed by Congress March 23, 1971. Ratified July 1, 1971.

(Amendment 14, section 2, of the Constitution was modified by section 1 of the 26th amendment.)

Section 1.

The right of citizens of the United States, who are eighteen years of age or older, to vote shall not be denied or abridged by the United States or by any State on account of age.

Section 2.

The Congress shall have power to enforce this article by appropriate legislation.

AMENDMENT XXVII

Originally proposed Sept. 25, 1789. Ratified May 7, 1992.

No law, varying the compensation for the services of the Senators and Representatives, shall take effect, until an election of representatives shall have intervened.

NOTES

NOTES

NOTES